Family
Fortunes

Family Fortunes

Chris Hudson

Illustrations by Peter Wilks

The National Society
A Christian Voice in Education

a co-publication with
Church House Publishing

The National Society/Church House Publishing
Church House
Great Smith Street
London SW1P 3NZ

ISBN 0 7151 4924 5

Published 1999 by the National Society (Church of England) for Promoting Religious Education and Church House Publishing

Cover illustration by Peter Wilks and cover design by Stuart Squires (SGA illustration agency, Hadleigh, Suffolk 1P7 5AP)

Printed in England by Biddles Ltd, Guildford and King's Lynn

Contents

Acknowledgements

Grateful thanks are due to the following:

Rachel, Jenny and Matthew, for giving me a lot of practical experience where it really counts.

Margaret and Trevor Cooling and all involved at the Stapleford Project, for support, encouragement and advice.

Hamish Bruce and all at Church House Publishing, for seeing it through from seedbed to harvest.

The Jerusalem Trust, for making it all possible.

Diane Parkin, for fanning the spark.

The staff, governors and children of Greysbrooke Primary School, Shenstone, for allowing it to happen in their time and on their premises.

The staff and children of the following schools:

Hatchford (GM) Primary School, Chelmsley Wood

Walmley (GM) Junior School, Sutton Coldfield

Hill West Junior School, Sutton Coldfield

Glenmead Junior/Infant School, Great Barr

St Andrew's Benn (CE) Primary School, Rugby

St Matthew's Bloxam (CE) Primary School, Rugby

While expressing my thanks for all the help and support given by the above, I think it only fair to add that any mistakes or errors in the text are my own.

This project has been supported by The Jerusalem Trust, one of the Sainsbury Family Charitable Trusts.

Introduction

*'I once used to have three theories for raising children.
I now have three children, and no theories.'* (Anon.)

*'Families are like aeroplanes.
You only hear about the ones that crash.'* (Anon.)

This book is a collection of stories, poetry and ideas for use with the 7–11 age group. The collective theme is 'families', families of all shapes and sizes. Very few of them come close to our modern idea of the 'nuclear family' of Dad, Mum and 2.4 children, but they are all based on Bible narratives or Bible themes on the subject of family life.

Children and their perceived needs absorb a great deal of our society's time, effort and attention. This book is intended to get them talking about families, thinking about what it means to be a member of a family, and making a positive contribution to their own family life. Children are not passive sponges absorbing the best that we can give, but actors and deliberators in their own right. Without the encouragement to see imaginatively the bigger picture that involves other people's needs and wants, they may remain content with the smaller picture – their own needs and wants. Stories (and poems) enable them to see their own impulses and dilemmas articulated, expressed and played out to a logical conclusion, and encourage debate of personal issues at a safe distance. Jesus repeatedly used narratives and pictures like this when teaching crowds – it probably carried a greater impact. A good story or poem can plant the seed of an idea in a child's mind that will have an enormous impact on their life when they are older – so handle them carefully!

Each story is accompanied by a teacher's page that summarizes the aims of the unit, suggests prompts to aid storytelling, and provides a range of differentiated activities for reinforcing the major ideas covered in RE and PSE, including worksheets. An additional section contains suggestions for using the photocopied story or associated poetry for literacy development.

There are two types of story here. Some are straight retellings of narratives from the Bible. I have tried not to take liberties with the text, aiming only to insert events that could reasonably have happened – such as the events surrounding the disappearance of the young Jesus in 'Going back'. Other stories take a biblical theme and play it out in a human situation – such as 'Homework', which provides opportunities for discussing what it actually means to 'love', and three stories set during other time periods: the Tudors, the Victorians and the Second World War. In each case, the setting provides a useful stage to play out an age-old dilemma in an unfamiliar setting.

Why have I used these particular stories? The aim has been to cover a range of themes common to family life. Several stories deal with feelings such as 'anger', while others go for an issue, such as 'growing up'. A great many conflicts in the home derive from either the inappropriate expression of strong emotion, or the inability to handle new dilemmas. Children can be helped if these issues are discussed away from the home in a secure, more neutral setting, and also if these issues are tackled in a positive way. How we think and learn will affect a great deal of what we do!

The source of inspiration for this book is the Christian Bible. Despite the strong differences between ancient understandings of 'family' and our own more individualized versions, the Bible has a great deal to offer in terms of insight and understanding into how people operate. As Mark Twain once said, 'Most people are bothered by those passages in Scripture which they cannot understand. The Scripture which troubles me most is the Scripture I do understand.'

Not all of our families are happy, but neither were all the families of the Bible. Not all of our family problems can be solved with a judicious piece of biblical wisdom – but the basic principles of love, fairness and commitment as demonstrated in the Bible still work, despite the enormous changes in society and culture that have taken place since the times when it was written. One obvious shift in understanding since biblical times has been the way that society views women. 'The quiver of arrows' tries to balance the ambiguities of applying a biblical idea to a contemporary setting, with modern ideas of social justice.

Please note that despite their sources, none of the stories or lesson material assumes a level of Christian faith. (This is deliberate, as many children and teachers do not come from religious backgrounds.) However, they do explore what it means to have faith, not only in God, but in other people and in oneself as well. Here are some of the answers that Christians and Jews have given across the centuries to people's questions about families, relationships and God.

Making the most of this book

Each unit in this book is designed to be run as an oral storytelling session, followed by RE and PSE work that will remind the children of some of the basic content, enable them to reflect on some of the ideas expressed, and explore ways of applying them. Specific literacy activities are also provided to capitalize on each unit's potential for teaching language (see Appendix 3). The teacher's page in each unit provides a range of differentiated ideas for follow-up – you, as the classroom teacher, need to pick and choose the most suitable material for the age of your class and their ability groups, from the activities and worksheets provided. There are two worksheets for each unit. The first worksheet will enable follow-up in RE and PSE, and the second will support follow-up using related Bible passages. Both are intended to be accessible to children of a wide range of ability, but younger children and some older children with special needs will need support in the form of prompts, word lists or extra discussion in a small group. Extension material is provided on the teacher's page.

Each unit will give you material for several lessons, so please don't feel that you have to cram it all into one session – the children will feel rushed, and you will get frustrated! Some of the material lends itself to use in different subjects. Consider the possibility of integrating some of your RE, PSE, literacy, music, history or other subjects if you are still able to fulfil your set programmes of study using the units. You may wish to photocopy the stories for children to refer to during follow-up work, but it may not be necessary, if your storytelling was sufficiently memorable! If you are going to revisit the content of a story over several sessions, then your special needs children may benefit from having an adult reader with them, or having the story committed to audiotape. It will also help them if you simplify the worksheets by providing word lists as prompts, and enlarged copies of the text with sections for study already highlighted. Some of the tasks might also best be attempted on a small-group or class basis as you see fit.

Using the stories: some helpful hints

1.   Read the story through to yourself beforehand, with that unit's teacher notes. Get a feel for its tone and pace. Each character in a story (and there aren't many, deliberately) should speak slightly differently. Have a sense for their age, their class

and their background. Look for clues in the text. Make the characters live in your imagination, so you can convey them as living beings to your audience. The small asterisks in the text (*) are suggested places to pause for discussing the story so far with your audience ('What's he feeling now? What do you think's going to happen next?' etc.). Use these if it fits your storytelling style.

2.   Prepare your classroom and audience. If you can, have children sitting on the floor together, but not squashed. Try to avoid moving lots of furniture just beforehand and be ruthless with distractions, all the way up to placing a 'Please Do Not Disturb for 15 minutes' sign on the door. (Do explain why, to the Head!) Prepare a small display to give eyes something to focus on – each unit of work in this book comes with ideas for visual prompts: pictures or artefacts that you can point to or hold up to maintain imaginative interest. Use your school reward system to reward good listeners in your class – and tell them you're going to do so beforehand! To aid recollection, list key words or names on the board as prompts to jog memory afterwards.

Follow-up activities

Be clear in your differentiation. Regardless of ability, each child should be given the opportunity to show that they are able to understand the basics of the story, reflect on its meaning and apply it in some way.

Each story is accompanied by a range of activities for reinforcing the major ideas covered in RE and PSE, with extension activities for exploring further. The following icons indicate a differentiation and a resource implication:

 Special needs

 Main body of class

 Extension activities for the more able

 Bible or portions of Bible text needed

Using the Bible

You will definitely need copies of the Bible (or portions of Bible texts, provided in Appendix 5) in a good modern child-friendly translation (see below for recommendations), so that some of the biblical ideas can be accessed, and so that children are given a chance to compare the stories with their originals. Appendix 5 provides you with the basic passages, but there is no substitute for the real thing! If your school does not have any Bibles and there is a problem with funding, consider (with your Head's approval) asking local Christian church congregations to sponsor the purchase of a school set – they may be only too pleased to help!

Children need to be shown how to handle Bibles, but it is not in the Christian tradition to venerate the actual book in the way that Muslims do the Qur'an. The children will need to be told that the Bible is a very special book to millions of people around the world, and as such it should be respected and looked after, like any precious family possession. However, they also need to be taught how to use a Bible, and most Christians would find nothing wrong with using a variety of games and drills to show children how to access particular passages. In fact, if your class are new to it and you have a class set of Bibles, then take a class lesson to explore the book with them. It may save you a lot of time later!

Exploring the Bible as a class activity

Decide on a passage, then, having given out the Bibles, all open the front cover. Work your way together through the first few pages until you find the Contents. Explain that the Bible is actually a collection of 66 books, and that the Contents page lists all the titles. Pick out the name of the book you are after. Find its page number. (Discussion of four-digit numbers may be needed at this point!) Then all find the book together, and explain that, to make life easier, somebody invented a way of finding a particular part of the book without ploughing through all the pages – they created the chapter-and-verse system. So, all together, find the right chapter, and then the right verse. Explain how the notation of chapter and verse works (title of book/chapter number/verse number, as in 'Job 28.1–28'), then set them off on a hunt to find another passage. Children can find this rather fun, and you could set the more able the task of finding a few choice passages such as:

● the 'Godzilla' passage (Job 41.1-34, referring to the mythical creature Leviathan);

● David and Goliath (1 Samuel 17.1-58);

● Gideon's battle (Judges 7.1-25);

● time for everything (Ecclesiastes 3.1-8).

If your class Bibles have one, then point out and investigate the index at the back as well. A good place to look would be the 'Parables of Jesus' – then see what comes up! Point out that, to save time, names of books in the Bible are often abbreviated (Mark becomes 'Mk', the first book of Kings becomes '1 Kings'), but they should be able to find a 'key' if in difficulty.

Recommended modern translations of the complete Bible include:

Children's International Version, Nelson Word, 1991, ISBN 1 860 24087 9

New Light Children's Bible, Hodder and Stoughton, 1996, ISBN 0 340 6870 7

Rainbow Good News Bible, Bible Society, 1994, ISBN 0 005 12842 0

The Bible for Children: New Jerusalem Version, DLT, 1996, ISBN 0 232 52149 2

Recommended versions using simpler language or partial extracts:

S. Hastings, *Children's Illustrated Bible*, Dorling Kindersley, 1997, ISBN 07513 5113X

B. Hartman, *Lion Storyteller Bible*, Lion, 1995, ISBN 0 7549 2921 4

A. Dilling, *Kingfisher Bible*, Kingfisher, 1993, ISBN 185697 1155

M. Batchelor, *Children's Bible in 365 Stories*, Lion, 1995, ISBN 0 7459 1333 4

The wider curriculum

These materials are intended to be used in a variety of ways: all the pages are photocopiable, and teachers may find that this enables some of the stories, poems and activities to be used as extension work in guided reading for the more able (for which suggestions are made in the teacher's notes for each unit), and as a basis for further work in literacy, speaking and listening, and drama. You can find more information on linking these units into your school's literacy programme in Appendix 3, along with some thoughts on developing the writing of poetry. You may find that your religious education lessons begin to dove-tail into other subject areas such as history (see below). This is as it should be, providing that you don't allow the mechanics of historical research (or whatever) to sideline the positive work with spiritual and moral values for which this book is primarily intended. Good RE enables every child to express themselves on an issue to their own satisfaction, even though sometimes it may not be to yours!

History

The following units could be used to accompany project work as part of your history curriculum:

Unit 2 includes the story 'Payback time' which provides a useful introduction to studying the Egyptians or Peoples of the Past. (It helps to use Unit 1 first as this provides contrast.)

Unit 5 includes the story 'The battle' which could be used to accompany work on Tudor England, the Renaissance, the Reformation and the Age of Discovery (1450–1700).

Unit 6 includes the story 'The ration book' which looks at Britain since 1930 to the twentieth century.

Unit 7 includes the story 'The quiver of arrows' which provides an introduction to Victorian Britain and life in Victorian times (for example, it opens up the subjects of the role of women and Victorian education).

UNIT 1
A family at war

It was a cold night. They often have them in Palestine. The group of men were huddled together around the camp fire at the bottom of the valley, keeping an eye now and then on the shepherd boys guarding hundreds of sheep and goats. The whole valley was full of the noise of their animals. Somebody said there were bandits about, and you had to be careful. Still, it was nothing to worry about. These men knew how to handle themselves in a fight. One or two had killed people before now.

Somebody started passing a bottle round the circle. There was nothing else to do. Dan was talking.

'I don't know what's got into the old man! I just don't! We're the ones who run the business. We're the ones who spend all our time chasing wolves and what have you, just so HE can sit in the lap of luxury back home!'

'True! It's not fair!' That was Simeon talking. 'The old man's losing his touch.

We know the sheep-and-goats business like the back of our hands and he still treats us like dirt, and we're the ones who are making it pay!'

They all grunted in agreement. Simeon kept talking.

'What gets me, what really gets me, is how he treats you, Reuben!' There was a nodding of heads. 'You're the eldest. You'll take over when the old man goes, we all know that, that's the way it's supposed to happen, but you wouldn't know it if you were an outsider coming in! They'd take one look around the camp back home, and see who's got the old man's ear, and they'd know. They'd see who the old man's grooming to take over!'

'Joseph!' they all muttered.

'Yes, Joseph! At his daddy's side every day. "Can I do this for you, Dad? Can I do that?" It makes me sick!' Simeon paused. He knew he was only saying what the others were thinking. Then he said the one thing that everybody knew, but no one had the nerve to say.

'It's Joseph's mum, really, isn't it? That's what it's all about. All right, so the old man's had several wives. That's life. We're all still brothers, and he's our dad. But it was Joseph's mum he really loved, and now she's dead he wants her son to run the business and not us. He looks at him and sees her. And the rest of us can just . . . go hang!' Simeon stared into the fire. It crackled in the embarrassed silence.*

'That's enough.' It was Reuben, the eldest.

'What do you mean?'

'I said it was enough. You've said your piece. Now leave it.'

'You're scared.' The drink was making Simeon bolder. 'You could run the family now with your eyes shut. Maybe they're shut already. Can't you see what's going on?' It all happened in a flash. Reuben leaped over the fire and with a shove, forced Simeon back down on the ground. He stood over him, a dark, menacing shadow.

'I said to leave it!' he growled. Simeon, shaken, stared up at the shadow, and nodded.*

'What's all this, then?' There was only one person who could speak in that high irritating voice. 'Fighting among yourselves? It must be boring up here with nothing to do.'

Everybody turned. Simeon, who was still lying down, pinned under Reuben's foot, looked sideways at Joseph, then up at Reuben.

'Look who it isn't. Daddy's little boy.' He grinned as Reuben let him up.*

'Nice to see you, brother,' he grunted at the newcomer as he dusted himself down. 'Any news from the camp?'

Joseph had sat down by the fire. 'Oh, nothing much. Father's sent me to see how things are doing. You weren't where you said you were going to be.'

Reuben was sitting facing him. 'That's because the old man sent us to a place where we've heard there's sheep-stealing going on, and there's not enough water. Here it's sheltered and there's water. Any objections?'*

Joseph didn't notice the danger. 'Who made the decision?'

'I did.'

'Father won't like that.' There was silence. Reuben was staring very hard at Joseph, who had started poking the fire with a stick.*

'Oh well . . . here's a funny thing. I keep having these dreams about all of us, and about Father. I don't know what they mean. Shall I tell you about them?' Nobody said anything. They'd heard them before.

'All right then. We were all out in the fields at harvest time. You know, cutting the corn, stacking it in sheaves to dry.' Simeon sniffed. Joseph hadn't got his hands dirty in a long time, not since he'd been given a special set of new clothes by his daddy, the set he was wearing now.

'We'd all made our sheaves and then . . . it happened.'

'What happened?' asked Simeon, all innocence. He knew this was going to be good. He'd actually heard about these dreams already. Joseph had talked about these dreams to lots of people, but not to his brothers like this, not miles from home, miles from Daddy.

'All the sheaves fell down, and mine didn't. In fact, it stood up, and the others seemed to be bowing down to it. What do you think it means, Reuben?' Reuben just stared.*

'Then I had another dream. I was standing on a mountain, and there was the sun and the moon . . . and eleven stars. And they all bowed down to me. I can't think what it means.'*

Your death, thought Simeon. You're not going to leave this place alive. Nobody spoke.

'Oh well, I'll just go for a walk. It's a nice night for it.' Joseph slipped out of the firelight. Wonderful, thought Simeon. He must have a death wish.

Time to make my move, thought Simeon. But it was another brother who spoke. Asher had stayed silent up to now. He spoke slowly.

'I say we kill him. Do it now, just the way we did with that scum who insulted our sister.'

'Kill him? How?' Simeon was interested.*

'Anything. A knife. A rock. Then shove him down a well and leave him for the wolves and buzzards. That's where his dreams can go.'

That's good, thought Simeon. I like that. Time for action. He stood up.

'I'm with you, brother! It's for our family!'

'And me!'

'Me too!'

The others stood up one by one. They were all going to be in on it, all except Reuben, who was now staring at the fire. He was looking at the flames.* He'd been listening, but he was thinking about his own dreams of leading the family, running the family business – and how Simeon was right. Joseph was going to take over, the way things stood. But to kill your brother . . . what would it do to the old man? If he said 'no' to his brothers, would they do it anyway? Asher might, if Simeon pushed him hard enough.

They were all looking at him. Now for it. Only one thing to do.

'No!' He stood up, a little uncertainly. 'I mean yes!'

'What?' They all crowded round, except Asher, who had drawn his knife and was looking at it closely.

'No blood! No killing! Just blindfold him, stick him in a well, any well. Then leave him. That way, there's no blood on our hands. We'll just . . . leave him there.'

Asher was looking disappointed. The others were obviously listening to big brother. As he saw the knife being placed back in its sheath, Reuben could see a way out of this. They could leave Joseph, move on, and then he'd come back, pull him out and send him home. The blindfold would stop him from seeing who had done it. It could happen! And nobody would have to die.*

He gave instructions, and they all fanned out up the valley. Where was the brat? There! Wearing a coat like that, you could see him from miles away! It all happened quickly. Simeon had the sack and Dan the rope. They crept up. Joseph was standing still, looking up at the stars.* What's he expecting? thought Simeon. They leapt. Simeon rammed the sack over Joseph's head, Dan grabbed his hands and tied them. Joseph yelled, but nobody who could help was listening. Without speaking they dragged him, kicking but helpless, down towards a disused well.

Asher was waiting there, his knife drawn in welcome. Just as they were going to throw him in, Joseph started screaming something about his Mum. Dan hit him and whispered some horrible threat in his ear, telling him to just stand there . . . or else, while Asher cut the coat off Joseph's back and arms, cutting the boy too, drawing blood and not caring about it. It only took a few seconds and their hooded victim was soon ready.

'One, two, three . . .' Dan pushed Joseph over the edge, and listened. There was a scuffling sound, then a satisfying thump at the bottom. That's him sorted, thought Simeon.*

Next morning, they broke camp and headed out of the valley. 'It's time to find new grazing for the sheep,' said Reuben to the servants. Everybody had their jobs to do, and nobody said anything about Joseph, although they all knew where he was. As the shepherds marshalled the flocks down, Reuben was careful to look back, marking the distant well in his memory. He'd be back that night with a rope.

Meanwhile, Asher had dipped the rags that used to be Joseph's coat in the blood of a goat that had been slaughtered and cooked for lunch. 'It's to make it more realistic when we say what happened – we can say that a wolf got him!' he grinned. Reuben didn't like the way these ideas came so easily to Asher.*

It was a busy day on the move with thousands of animals, and they'd stopped when they met some Arab traders who were interested in doing a little buying and selling. Reuben really had to insist before everyone started moving again. He knew that his brother Judah had made some sort of deal with the Arabs, because they'd given him some money before moving off, twenty shekels in silver coins. Odd that, thought Reuben. What was he selling?

He found out that night when he had ridden back to the well. Joseph was missing. Did he untie himself and escape?

'Oh no!' said Judah back at camp, when Reuben demanded to know what had happened. 'I thought – why does the little whatsit have to die? All we wanted to do was get rid of him, so I thought, let's sell him! He'll live. He just won't be living with us, and that's what we all want, isn't it? No blood, no killing. You should be pleased!'

My own brother sold into slavery! Reuben was terrified. What would their father say if he ever found out?*

Unit 1
Teacher's notes

 ● To consider anger and envy as strong feelings, and the issues that can cause them, such as insensitivity and lack of 'fairness';

● To consider ways of positively handling the feelings and the issues.

 Sheepskin rug, pictures/models of sheep, bright coloured dressing gown or robe.

Reinforcement of the biblical story

1. What did the brothers dislike about Joseph? List as many things as you can, but try to think why these things made them cross. Draw the family with their comments in thought bubbles.

2. What choices did Reuben have at different points in the story? Why did he act the way he did? Write about his choices.

3. What do you think Reuben and Joseph are feeling at the end of this part of the story? Do you think they would have any regrets? What parts of this story do you think they would want to change if they could? Start your writing with the words, 'I remember . . .' or 'I wish . . .'

(As above, but in cartoon form with thought bubbles.)

4. Compare the original Bible story of Joseph (Genesis 37, see p. 104) with the colloquial retelling. What's been changed? What's the same? Why has the author told it like this?

PSE

Anger

1. Lots of people get angry in this story. Design a red 'angry' monster to show the things that really make you mad.

2. Certain things in the story don't seem to be fair. People sometimes say 'It's not fair!' What does 'fair' mean? Try to arrive at a class definition. Create mini-cartoons on 'Fairness is . . .' along the lines of the 'Love is . . .' cartoons.

3. There's a lot of anger in the story. It is sometimes right to feel angry if you or someone else is being treated badly, but anger often leads people to do wrong things, such as resorting to violence. What are the right ways and the wrong ways of expressing anger? Discuss this as a group or class, then create cartoon posters conveying the message 'Don't let your anger lead you into wrong.'

Insensitivity

4. Joseph was insensitive to the feelings of others. He didn't seem to notice that he was making people angry, until it was too late. Create a class list of 'world's worst' and 'world's best' things to say to someone:

who is very upset;

who's been told off for not working hard enough;

who is scared of the dark.

(As above, but with prompts on board generated by discussion.)

Envy

5. Watch a video clip from a TV advert or find a magazine advert that encourages envy, then discuss the meaning of envy. Look up definitions in different dictionaries. Many advertisements play on our envy in a bid to make us buy things: 'If I buy that make-up, I will look like that person.' Design an advert for a totally stupid product that plays on our sense of envy ('"Eat crispy chicken-feet and you'll look like an Imperial Stormtrooper!" says Darth Vader!'), or design a green 'envy' monster that shows all the things that others have that you want.

Drama work

Warm up then brainstorm some family situations that illustrate the following in the home: **anger, insensitivity, envy**. Ask the children to create a 'freeze-frame' situation in small groups, where each plays a character in a situation. In turn, ask each group to 'freeze' in a pose, then go round asking each character who they are and what they would be feeling in this situation. For example:

Anger – an argument over bedtimes.

Who are you? – 'I'm a big brother'

What do you feel? – 'Fed up. My little sister goes to bed at 8.00, and they still expect me to go to bed at 8.30!'

Insensitivity – an argument over whose turn it is to wash up.

Who are you? – 'I'm the mother'

What do you feel? – 'I just wish they would stop arguing and help me.'

Envy – feelings about unfairness on Christmas Day morning.

Who are you? – 'I'm her little brother'

What do you feel? – 'I'm cross about my sister. She's got better Christmas presents than me!'

Then, to be positive, turn the situations around with illustrations of what would be the opposite to envy, anger and insensitivity. Any ideas? For further developments along this line, create a little soap opera (using characters from TV) to illustrate these ideas.

Literacy work

1.   Study the original conversations of the brothers around the campfire. How does what they say give you clues about the sort of people they are? Study how Simeon and Reuben speak before Joseph appears. Brainstorm some words to describe the way they talk. Now create a conversation in a similar style that could take place in your playground. What could the two people be arguing about?

2.   Collect words on the theme of anger, jealousy and envy. One way to do it is to play 'The Furniture Game' where you describe something in terms of the characteristics of something else. ('If being angry was an animal, what kind of animal would it be? If it was a colour/plant/sound/place/etc., what kind of . . . would it be?') Use the resulting lists to create symbolic poems about that emotion. ('Anger is a growling roaring red lion . . .')

3.   Read the poem 'Ice' (see p. 83). It starts with a person saying what they are thinking, but their thoughts change – can you see at which point? Create a piece of writing (poetry or prose) where one person is talking (or thinking aloud), but they're not quite sure if what they are thinking is right, and we can see the person's thoughts changing. This kind of writing is called a monologue. Subjects could include: 'The reason I hate my brother', 'I've never got enough pocket money', or 'My football team is rubbish'.

A family at war

WORKSHEET 1

Name_____   **Date** _____

Next to the cross face, write *four* things that the brothers disliked about Joseph.

_____

_____

_____

_____

Reuben makes a choice in the story. Write what Reuben did in the first bubble.

Write what action he could have taken in the second bubble.

A family at war

WORKSHEET 2

Name_____   **Date** _____

Read the original version of this story in the Bible in Genesis 37.1-36.

Then answer the following:

Jacob's family is very unhappy, and things are going badly. How will the following people in this story have to change if this family is going to solve its problems and live together peacefully? *Why* will they have to change?

Jacob   _____
           _____
           _____
           _____

Joseph   _____
           _____
           _____
           _____

Brothers _____
           _____
           _____
           _____

UNIT 2

Payback time

Egypt had style, he had to admit it. Reuben had only been here once, and he'd never made it this far before. His family had travelled and traded in wool and livestock for hundreds of years, but it had never meant actually having to travel into the kingdom of the Egyptian Pharaoh. Reuben didn't really trust foreigners. He always thought they were trying to put one over on him. Out in the desert, it didn't matter, because everyone was trying to do much the same thing. You were all the same there, haggling over this number of sheep and that number of bales of wool. He'd met Egyptians before, of course, but only merchants and traders like himself. It was different, travelling right into the capital city of a foreign country.

Even the smells were different – and the buildings, massive palaces and pyramids and statues of giants that must have lived long ago before the Flood! There were statues of strange gods with animal heads that made him feel rather sick. He'd heard about what the Egyptians did with their dead, of course, but it was strange seeing it all going on around you.

The River Nile was another sight that astonished him – all that water in one place, slowly pouring out to sea! The Nile Valley was even more incredible miles and miles of barren trees and fields. The village markets were still full of food – beautiful sweet-smelling breads, cakes and pastries laden with dried fruit and spices! Reuben felt dizzy from all the sights and sounds and smells. His own country of rough hills and mountains seemed a million miles away, but he wanted to be there instead. This place wasn't for him.*

The Prime Minister's palace was big, just like everything else in Egypt. This was where the journey ended. Reuben and his brothers were making a special visit to buy food. Things were bad back home, what with the famine and everything.

They were standing in the entrance hall of the palace, waiting for someone to see them. The room was cool. They'd been allowed to wash and groom themselves and put on their best robes, just so they could make a good impression. Reuben gazed around at the wall paintings and statues. This Prime Minister of theirs must be pretty rich, he thought.

'They say he's the one who really runs Egypt, you know.'

'What?' Reuben turned to Judah, who was studying a painting of an Egyptian god with a jackal's head, holding a whip.

'This Prime Minister. They say he's more important than Pharaoh. It's like he's the one who does the bookkeeping. I heard that he owns all the corn in Egypt, and he'll only sell it for gold.'

'Let's just hope he takes silver, then. It's all we've got.'

'Speaking of which, have you got the present?'

'All here, nicely washed and pressed. He'll love it.'

'He'd better. If our family's going to have a future, he's got to like it.'

There was a cough. A door had opened silently, and a shaven-headed official had appeared out of nowhere. He bowed, and pointed the way they should go. The brothers got in line. Reuben felt sick, but didn't want it to show.*

'Off we go, lads. Try not to spit on the floor. Remember, impress him!'

Impress him? Good grief, he sniffed. We're a bunch of herdsmen who can't even wash the stink of sheep out of our hair. The biggest thing we've built is a tent. Look at us! Look at this place! It's all we can do just to not tread on each other's feet!

The corridor opened out into a long hall. At the end stood a shining throne flanked by statues of more gods and a few real live servant girls waving fans. The throne was empty, but waiting for someone special. Reuben glanced around in amazement. Everywhere, the gleam of gold, the sparkle of fine jewellery.

'Don't look at him when he comes in. It's bad manners!' whispered the official. Reuben adjusted his eyes downwards. 'Approach the throne with head bowed. At the far end, you get down on your knees if you want to impress. If he gives permission, you may look up. Best of luck!'

'Why?'

'He's having a bad day. We've executed three spies already!'

'Er . . . thanks.'

The brothers stood there, dead still. There was a shuffling in the corridor outside, a ripple of small bells, and the Prime Minister strode in, reading from a roll of papyrus.* He grunted as he sat on the throne, took his time to finish reading, then looked up.

'Well?' He had a hard face. A servant spoke.

'Merchants, your Excellency, from Palestine, here to buy grain.'

'With what?' He stared at the brothers. Reuben felt naked. He bowed and stepped forward.

'With silver and woollen goods, Your Excellency. We have heard that you sell at a fair price to all in need.' He felt extremely uncomfortable. Oh well, nothing for it but keep to what they'd planned. 'As a token of our great esteem, we have brought a gift for your most gracious Excellency.' He nodded to Dan, who brought forth one of the robes on a hanger.

'A woollen coat with full sleeves and embroidered trimmings, only given to the most especially valued of our people.' Dan was holding the coat up for all to see. 'The wool is spun by our women and coloured using natural dyes created to a secret recipe guarded since time began. Your Excellency, this coat will keep you warm in the winter and cool in the summer when you ride out on your chariot.'

The room was silent. Reuben was sweating. Was he saying the right things? The Prime Minister was staring straight at him! Reuben looked down in embarrassment, then noticed that the Prime Minister's hands were shaking. Had he said something wrong? There was a shuffle, the Prime Minister was standing, then walking, half-running out of the room. More silence. What had he said? A servant coughed. 'Er, this audience is at an end. Please return to the entrance hall and await His Excellency's pleasure.'*

'This way,' said a voice by his side, and he allowed another servant, the shaven-headed one, to lead him out. Was that it? This country and its people must be stark-staring mad!

Meanwhile, in a small room nearby, the Prime Minister was half-muttering and half-sobbing to himself as he stared at the ceiling.

'It's them! After all these years it's them! God in heaven, what's going on? It's them! And they've even brought along a coat like the old one! Do they know? No, of course not, they couldn't . . . but they're here, in my palace!'*

Joseph thought of summoning the guards, clapping them in irons, throwing them in prison and hurling away the keys into the waters of the Nile. Revenge! His eyes lit up. He could pay them back for all they'd done! All those wasted years as a slave, as a prisoner! Oh, this was going to be good, so good!

'Thank you, God!' he spluttered. 'I can get my own back on the family that sold me into slavery! Yes! I can pay them back! Pay them back!' He was almost spitting with rage. He didn't know what he wanted to do. All those memories flooded back, all the anger, all the pain. Yes, he was going to do something, all right. They were in his power at last. He'd show them.*

Then he thought about his father and Benjamin. Where were they? Were they still alive? Had his brothers killed them? He had to know more! His desire for revenge had evaporated. Straightaway, he thought of a plan.

A few minutes later, the servant appeared by Reuben's shoulder. 'His Excellency will see you now.'

The brothers lined up again, Dan still holding the coat, unsure whether to wrap it up again or not. ('Hang it over your arm!' said Reuben, exasperated.) In they trooped to the long hall again, a little more confident now, having been in there once already. These Egyptians must be crazy.

This time, the Prime Minister was on his throne, staring at them as they marched up to him, this mad foreigner. There was a long pause.

'You are SPIES!' he shouted. Oh no, thought Reuben. 'Yes, SPIES!' He must like the word, he kept saying it. 'You've come to see where our land is unprotected!' Reuben had to say something, anything.

'No, my lord! We've just come to buy food. Like we said, we're all of us sons of one man, not spies!'

The Prime Minister glared. 'All ten of you? Your father is a remarkable man!'

Then Dan decided to chip in. 'He is! There used to be twelve of us – one's stayed with our dad, the other had an accident and died!' Reuben cringed.*

The Prime Minister rose from his throne. They'd fallen into his trap. 'Then prove it! Send for your brother, and we'll see if his story is the same as yours. Meanwhile, you will remain here at my pleasure.' He clapped his hands. 'Guards! Away with them!'

That night, sitting on the prison floor, Reuben felt like stuffing the whole coat down Dan's stupid throat.

Three days later, they were all summoned back to see the Prime Minister, who looked strangely satisfied and pleased to see them. Reuben didn't like his smile. There was a clap of hands and he looked up. What was going to happen?

'I have decided on a way to prove your story. One of you will stay as prisoner. The others will go with the grain . . .' he paused, ' . . . and fetch your younger brother. You may now discuss among yourselves who is to stay.' He sat back, watching and listening. How would they cope with that? He expected to see arguing, a bit of pushing and shoving, maybe a fist-fight, like in the old days. He used to enjoy starting an argument and then standing back to watch the punch-up.*

Today, it didn't happen. Judah was whispering to the others.

'It's a judgement, that's what it is. It's the blood of Joseph on our hands that's done this. We're all going to die because of what we did to him.'

'What about father?' muttered Asher. 'He'll die if Benjamin has to come. His heart won't take it.' He actually sounded worried.

Then Reuben spoke. 'I told you all not to kill the boy, but you wouldn't listen! We're going to have to pay for that blood, all of us! I told you!'

'I'll stay,' said Judah. He felt it was all his fault anyway. Joseph was astounded.*

'No! I'll stay! You're needed to handle the animals.' It was Simeon talking. Joseph was amazed. Simeon? This couldn't be the same Simeon who'd stitched him up all those years ago, who'd plotted to kill him! He had changed! They were all talking like men who actually cared about their father, and who knew they'd done wrong all those years ago!

There was more discussion, then Simeon shuffled forward, holding out his hands to be bound before being taken down to the cells.

They've changed, thought Joseph. They're not the people they used to be. I should be enjoying pushing them around, but I'm not. This wasn't how I planned it. They're different people now. They need help.

His plans for revenge were changing fast. Now he was thinking new plans. 'So they're starving in Palestine, are they?' he thought. Maybe he could help. A strange feeling came over Joseph as the guards took Simeon away, past his brothers who were patting him on the back and promising to return. For the first time in years, Joseph felt like crying.*

UNIT 2

Teacher's notes

 Aim To study the processes of reconciliation and coping with anger, using events from the life of Joseph as detailed in Genesis 42.1-24. To make any sense, this story should really be used as a follow-on from Unit 1!

 Prompts Pictures of Ancient Egypt, especially treasures and wall paintings from the tomb of Tutankhamen.

Reinforcement of the biblical story

1. List at least five different things that Reuben notices about life in Egypt, and explain why the brothers were visiting the country.

(Discuss, provide prompts on board.)

2. What clues does the author give you that the Prime Minister is powerful? How does this make the brothers feel?

3. How does Joseph realize that these traders are actually his brothers? What does he feel like doing to them when he realizes who they are? What is it that makes him put his desire for revenge to one side?

4. How does Joseph save his family from starvation and reveal who he really is? Research what happened next in the story, then retell that part in your own words. (You'll find it in the Bible in the book of Genesis, chapters 42 to 45. The author ended his version of the story at chapter 42, verse 24, see p. 106.)

PSE

(Appendix 1 of this book may be helpful when discussing some of the following material with your class.)

1. Discuss what 'anger' is. What sorts of things make people angry? How do they show it? Create a poster giving advice about managing your strong feelings and doing something positive about them. 'Don't let the sun go down on your anger' is old advice from the Bible about not allowing anger to go on and on. What do *you* think?

 (Discuss and list ideas in a small group first.)

2. Give your own definition of 'revenge'. Now look it up in a dictionary and copy out the dictionary definition. How does it compare with your version? What causes some people to try and 'get their own back'? Write a short story about somebody who seeks revenge.

3. Joseph had a lot to be angry about. In the story, he talks about his anger to God. Think about the person you talk to when you are angry. Write down the qualities of the sort of person you would talk to when angry.

4. It's hard to say sorry, and it's hard to forgive as well, but we all need to do that sometimes. Brainstorm a few ideas for showing someone there's no hard feelings. Design and make a 'Sorry' or 'I forgive you' card.

Literacy work

1.   All through the story, Egypt and its people are being described through the eyes of Reuben, someone who has never been there before. He notices all sorts of things. What does this tell you about him? Read through the story again, picking out the key words that describe what he notices, and the words that describe how he feels. Use these to help you create either a letter that Reuben could send home to his father, describing the land of Egypt and its people, or some pages in his personal diary. What will Reuben's feelings be as he describes each place and person? How will you convey this in his letter or diary?

2.   Summarize the main events of this story in a few good sentences, using exactly 100 words. You will need to prepare for this first, by re-reading the story and making notes. Be sure to include the names of all the major characters, and their reasons for acting the way they do.

3.   Read the poem 'Joseph' (see p. 82). List all the words that are meant to rhyme with each other. Which word is repeated in the last line of every verse? Why do you think this is? How does it affect the final message of the poem?

Payback time

WORKSHEET 1

Name_____   **Date**_____

1. List four different things that Reuben notices about life in Egypt.

_____

_____

_____

_____

2. How does this make Reuben feel? Circle one or more of the words below. (Can you add any more?)

worried	scared	anxious
curious	uninterested	excited
bored	puzzled	confused
_____	_____	_____

3. How does Joseph feel when he realizes that these traders are his brothers? Add at least three more words to the list below.

angry	powerful	upset
_____	_____	_____
_____	_____	_____

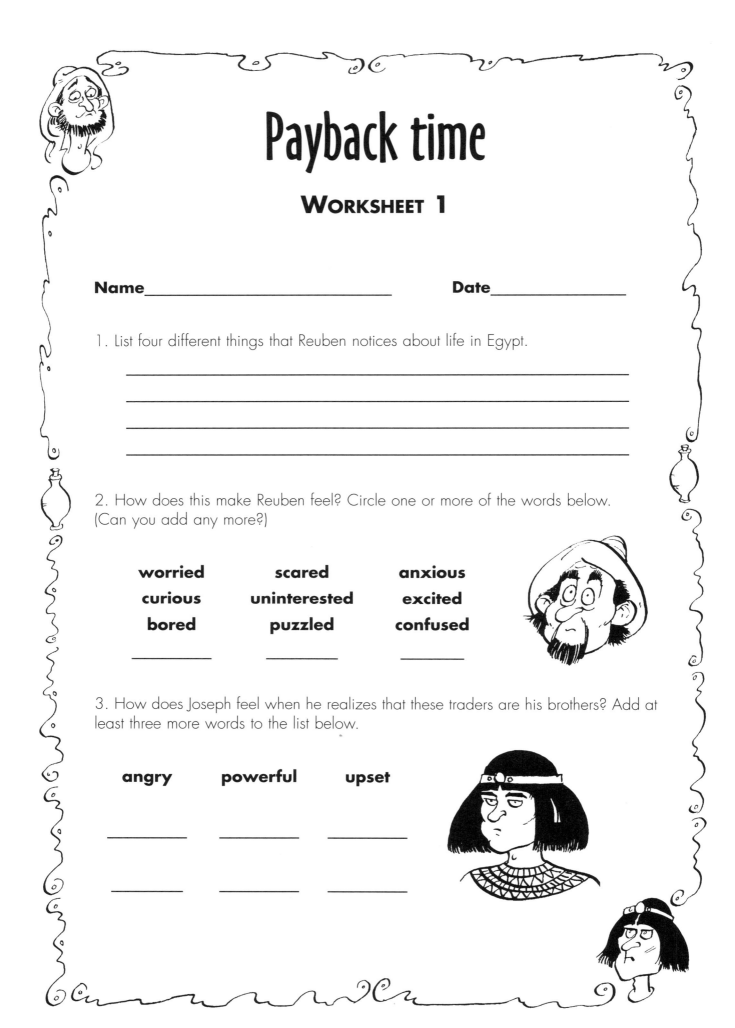

Payback time

WORKSHEET 2

Name_____   **Date**_____

Read the original version of this story in Genesis 42.1-24. Then answer the following.

1. In this part of the story, you can see that Joseph is a rather different person from what he used to be. How do you think he has changed?

_____
_____
_____
_____

2. How does he act when he first meets his brothers in Egypt?

_____
_____
_____

3. How does he react when he hears them talking about himself in their own language?

_____
_____
_____

4. Given Joseph's behaviour so far, what different things do you think he could do next?

_____
_____
_____
_____

UNIT 3
Going back

Joe raced down the street, calling out his son's name. 'Jeshua! Jeshua!' Several children turned, but none was him. 'Jeshua!' His voice echoed down the crowded alleyways, people glancing, some turning to stare, but most of them shrugging and carrying on with their little errands. He came to a cross-roads, looking left and right, trying to pick out one face among hundreds, one particular colour of tunic against all the other shades and patterns.

'Jeshua! Where are you?'

He looked for the creamy white tunic, the mop of tousled hair that always looked uncombed. Blast the boy! Whenever you wanted him, he was some-where else, the place you'd least expect! He wasn't like the other lads. Now James, his brother, he was different, a craftsman already at the age of ten, spending as much time as his Dad in the shop. You could tell how he'd turn out already, knocking out a nest of chairs as well as his Dad.

Jeshua, blast him! Where was he? Joe picked a direction, started to run down it, then stopped. This was useless. What had his own Dad always said? 'If you lose something, stop. Retrace your steps. Think.'

He found a bench and sat down. A waiter from a roadside bar came to take his order – would he like a drink? 'No . . . er, sorry . . . Yes, please.' He paid for the soft drink and sat sipping it, breathing slowly, in out, in out. 'Calm down.' That's what his old Dad would have said. His Dad had been a patient man, slow to anger, always good to turn to in a crisis, especially during that time when Joe had just got engaged. 'Think,' he'd say. 'Retrace your steps. It's the only way. Look for clues.' It had worked then – they'd sorted it out. Now he was on his own. Think! Remember!*

He remembered snatches of conversation, sights and smells of the last week. 'Look for the grain in the wood,' his Dad said. 'See where it leads.' His Dad was a typical woodworker, often starting a job not knowing how it would turn out, using the grain in the wood to make something that looked good and did the job, too. Think!

It was now three days that Jeshua had been missing. Three days! Three days of hell searching the streets of a massive city for one boy! Think! His mind wandered as a herd of camels were driven down the street, stinking of dung and the desert. Think! His mind drifted back over the last week, looking for clues.

He remembered the journey a week ago, almost half a village travelling as a caravan on wagons, on animals and on foot. Children were running up and down playing Tig, women were gossiping, men leading animals or keeping a close watch on the surrounding hills for bandits. The journey had felt safe – there was always safety in numbers when you were travelling. Mary and Elizabeth were swapping stories, Jeshua and his cousin John were off somewhere together, probably with another uncle.

Why was he remembering this? The boys. That was it. They'd been up the front of the caravan all the time, way out in front when they reached the crest of the hill. Those two were the first in the whole party to see Jerusalem.

'We're here! We're here!' they'd yelled, jumping up and down, then wrestling in the dust, laughing. More laundry, Joe had thought. He'd had to dismount, go and pick them up and pull them apart, but stopped when he'd seen the City of Gold. Everyone was stopping and staring as their destination came into sight. It was at that moment he'd known they'd made the right decision to go to Jerusalem for the celebration. Good old Zechariah. He'd fixed it so that Jeshua and Zechariah's son John could have their Bar Mitzvahs together in the Temple precincts, at a private party. (It was useful having a priest in the family.) Joe remembered his own Bar Mitzvah all those years ago, frowned, and then smiled – his own son's Bar Mitzvah had been everything he'd hoped for.

A waiter brought another drink. Where in this teeming city could his boy be? He fumbled for some change to pay the waiter, and found the little frankincense bottle that he normally kept around his neck. It was empty now. He'd kept it for years and then used it for a Temple sacrifice just the way he'd always promised himself, for celebrating his son becoming a man at his Bar Mitzvah. He thought back again. What an evening that was! The caterers were stacking tables with trays of kebabs, the musicians were tuning up, but in the meeting hall you could have heard a pin drop.

Jeshua and John were standing proudly on a raised platform facing the congregation, looking as if they owned the place. Joe's heart had been pumping, willing them to get it right. Don't drop the pointer! Take a deep breath before speaking! Zechariah had drilled the boys in exactly what they had to do. Now it was up to the boys to show they were ready to be treated as men, taking their place in the synagogue with the adults. All they had to do was read aloud from the scriptures, and make a little comment about what it meant. That's all. That's all? Joe had been terrified at his own Bar Mitzvah, but these two were perfectly relaxed. Are they too relaxed? Don't let us down, Jeshua! Joe gave his wife's hand a little squeeze. She smiled and squeezed him back. 'Why isn't she worried?' he'd thought.*

The boys hadn't let them down. They'd learned the whole passage off by heart, and took turns reading from Psalm 139, which was the passage the boys had chosen.

> You created every part of me;
> you put me together in my mother's womb.

Their clear voices echoed around the hall. My son's a man, thought Joseph. He's a man! Joe just wanted to stamp and clap and give three cheers. He knew it wasn't done, but then he stood and did it anyway, his big carpenter's hands slapping together. Everyone rose and joined in, yelling and whistling. The boys had done well.* On the platform, Jeshua and John grinned. At the back of his mind, Joe had seen that grin before, and it always meant trouble.

He sipped his drink, remembering the party and the presents (all brought from Nazareth, all going back there – daft!) and the dancing. It had been fantastic! Joe had even danced with Mary when no one was looking. What a night!* Then it was back to the inn, and sleep. Next day, they'd packed and headed back home, all the kids sharing rides with everyone else – everyone all over the place but travelling the same way. But not, it appeared, Jeshua.

Think! When did you last see him? The whole caravan had left, heading for the Beautiful Gate out of the city, by the covered market. He'd seen Jeshua and John riding a borrowed donkey, and then Jeshua was looking up and pointing. Mary had spotted something in the market and was just popping over to grab a bargain on a fruit stall. Then Joe had spotted a pickpocket, and then it was something else. They were all on the road and it was the end of the day before Mary had asked if he'd seen Jeshua.

The panic rose again in Joe. How stupid he'd been! How can you lose your own son?

'Another drink, sir?' The waiter was polite, so Joe bought another.

Where had they gone? If you've lost something, go back. Back? How far back? Nazareth? Bethlehem? He shuddered at the memory of how his first child was born, then looked at the empty frankincense bottle. Funny how it had all turned out.* He felt that the bottle was a clue, part of a children's puzzle that fitted together only one way.*

Go back. He finished the drink, stood, and headed down the street back to the last place he'd seen the boys, where they'd been riding that donkey. In a few minutes, he was on the spot and looked up. Yes, that's where they'd been pointing. The Temple! Joe ran.

On reaching the Temple precincts, he stopped. Where now? A hand touched his shoulder. He turned. Mary! She'd been searching too.

'Anything?' she asked.

'Maybe,' he said. She followed him into the Temple, pushing past the traders selling sacrifices and souvenirs. This was the place where they'd bought two doves all those years ago. Over there was the place where he'd gone with his little bottle to make that sacrifice a couple of days ago. Look, man, look! Where would they be? Retrace your steps!

Memories flooded back, of Bethlehem again, of strangers blundering in to see a baby, and gifts that bought safe passages to another country. Gold, myrrh and frankincense. He pulled out the bottle and stared at it again, trying in his imagination to squeeze the answer out of it. In his mind, the pieces of the puzzle were coming together. He was distracted by shouting.

In one corner of the courtyard, some students were arguing – some kind of open-air summer school where hotheads could safely let off steam. In the middle was a boy. Jeshua was standing, talking to the lecturer.

At last! Joe pushed through the crowd, reaching to grab his son by the scruff of the neck when a gentle hand touched him. Mary, again.

'Joe, he's a man now.'

'Men don't treat their parents like that,' he growled, too exhausted with worry to shout. He turned to Jeshua. 'Three days we've been looking for you! Three days! Don't you care?'

Jeshua was blushing, but when he spoke, it was confidently, just like at the Bar Mitzvah reading. 'Why didn't you look here first? This is my Father's house.' Of course, thought Joe. The Temple. That's what it was all about.

'My Father's house.' Jeshua hadn't said it rudely or defiantly, although it could have been, but the word 'Father' felt like a knife stuck in Joe's stomach. He knew (like no one else did) what Jeshua really meant. Jeshua was a man now. True, he had to be treated more like an equal, a child of God like all Jews. Everyone understood that, but Joe also knew something else. His son was no longer his. He belonged to someone else, another Father. That's why the boy had come to the Temple. It was his Father's house.*

Jeshua stepped forward and looked down at Joe. His face looked very young and very old at the same time. 'Sorry, Dad. I didn't mean it like that.' He turned to Mary. 'Sorry, Mum. Let's go home.'

Holding hands as a family, they made their way out of the Temple. There was a long way to go before evening.*

UNIT 3

Teacher's notes

 Aim To consider the importance of celebrating 'coming of age', and for parents to 'let go'.

This story is an extrapolation of possible events surrounding the incident recorded in Luke 2.41-52, when the boy Jesus went missing for three days. It includes the possibility that Jesus had his Jewish Bar Mitzvah celebrated in the same week, although we have no evidence that Bar Mitzvahs were being celebrated in this historical period. Jewish boys (and now some Jewish girls) currently undergo this ceremony on reaching the age of thirteen. The high point of the celebration comes when the boy reads aloud and comments from a Scripture passage to an assembled congregation of family and friends. This is, understandably, quite an ordeal – but it is a sign that the child is now ready to take their place in the adult congregation.

'Jeshua' is the Aramaic original (meaning 'God saves') of a name rendered by the Greeks as 'Jesus'.

 Prompts A large picture of Jerusalem (or any Middle Eastern city), a drink in a glass and a small unlabelled glass bottle. Pictures (or even a video) of a Jewish Bar Mitzvah will also help in explaining the ceremony.

Reinforcement of the biblical story

1. Joe remembers different things during his search for Jeshua. With drawings, create a photo album of some of his memories, including the final scene in this story, with captions explaining what they mean.

(Discuss first, ensuring that each of Joe's memories is understood to be part of a larger story that begins with the nativity of Jesus, then growing up in Nazareth, then the Bar Mitzvah. The worksheet will be made easier if the children are given the captions.)

2. List the good things that Joe felt about Jeshua growing up. Why did he feel them? What did he get cross about, and why?

(Make a class or group list first.)

3. Compare the Bible story (Luke 2.41-52, see p. 107) with the version written here. What's been added to the original story, and why?

4. Find out more about the Bar Mitzvah ceremony and create a small interactive display on the subject, with a set of questions that people can answer, using the display.

PSE

1. 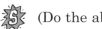 Make a chart showing what you could do in the past at different ages ('At five years old, I could . . .') and show what you would like to be able to do as you grow older ('At thirteen years old, I would like to . . .').

(Do the above, with drawings.)

2. How do people celebrate 'coming of age' now? Write about it, especially if you've been to a celebration.

3. Joe finds it hard to treat Jeshua as a man. Why do you think it was hard for him to do this? Do parents today still find it hard? What can children do to show that they can be treated as more grown up?

Literacy work

1. Write about what Jeshua had to do at his own Bar Mitzvah. How would you feel if *you* had to stand up and read to a large group of people? Why?

2. Joe has to do a lot of remembering in this story! A lot of the action takes the form of flashbacks. Can you find and list them all?

3. Each flashback is important to the story, because it builds up a picture of the sort of child Jeshua is. Study each flashback for clues. Make notes about the things you notice about Jeshua and then use them to write a character study of the boy. (What things are important to him? What sorts of things does he do? Would *you* like him if you met him?)

4. In the story, the boys use Psalm 139 as the reading at the Bar Mitzvah. Find a copy of this psalm and read it for yourself. It's written as a kind of prayer. Sum up what the writer is trying to say in about 100 words.

Going back

WORKSHEET 1

Name_____ **Date**_____

Joe's photograph album

1. Listen to or read the story. Draw some of Joe's early memories of Jeshua in the empty photographs and give them suitable captions underneath.

2. Under the smiley face, list Joe's good feelings about Jeshua growing up, and the things he finds difficult under the sad face.

Going back

WORKSHEET 1

Name_____ **Date**_____

Read the original story in Luke 2.41-52, then answer the following questions.

1. List three things that are different in the original story from the story you have heard. What has been added?

_____
_____
_____

_____
_____

2. Most of the stories about Jesus talk about his adult life. What do you think this original story from his childhood tells us about him? List at least three things around the picture.

3. What do *you* think the message of this story is? Write it in one sentence.

_____
_____

UNIT 4

The healer

It was the listening that she couldn't stand. Mary hated the sound of her brother's wheezy cough, the hard straining of breath in and out, in and out. It became easier for him at some points, and worse at others. Somebody had to sit with him, to hold his hand and encourage him – to let him know that there was someone else who knew how he felt. You couldn't just leave a young man to suffer by himself, not when he's family, not when he's your brother.

In . . . and out. In . . . and out. Mary had got used to the room, to the view from this chair. Her mind wandered when his breathing became easier. 'She could daydream for the Olympics,' her sister had said. Mary smiled. Martha was always like that. Every household needs a dragon, someone to make sure that everything happens; someone whose mind can carry a flood of thoughts at once. People like that get put in charge of things. Mary thought that Martha could organize and run the Olympics, given half a chance. She organized everything else in the village.

In . . . and out. In . . . and out. He seemed to be sleeping now, at rest. People forget how much hard work it is to be sick, she thought. You have to strain even to breathe; eating becomes a torture. You're weak at a time when you need to be strong. She felt that her brother was fighting with the infection that was tearing through his body; that parts of him were fighting little wars with invisible enemies. All he'd done was cut himself in his workshop, but the cut had gone bad, and now the disease was racking his whole body.*

There was a knock at the door. It was Martha. 'Is he still the same?'

Mary nodded, feeling his forehead. 'Getting colder, I think – but he's sleeping. The healer should be here soon, shouldn't he? Have you heard anything?'

'No,' stated Martha, flatly. 'You'd think he'd have sent word if he was coming, or even if he wasn't, he'd let us know. We sent a clear-enough message. "Come quickly, Lazarus sick, close to death." What else is there? He knows where we are, he knows who Lazarus is and he knows us. We wouldn't send for him if it wasn't important.' She paused. 'He should know it won't be a trap.'

It didn't reassure Mary. 'It's still too dangerous for him to come. People will be watching the roads. He could be arrested just for coming here.'

Martha shrugged. 'He'll come. He always goes where he's most needed – and that's here, now.'

'He'll be too late.' Mary was looking at the way Lazarus was breathing again.*

Martha was having none of this. 'Nonsense!' she snorted. 'Stop being so gloomy! He'll come – you'll see!' She stomped off to get some more towels. Mary didn't see. She knew how the roads were being watched. The healer had enemies who knew about his friendship with her family. He used to make surprise visits because he knew he would always be welcome here, but this was different. Mary could just imagine the conversations taking place behind closed doors.

'Oh, so Lazarus is sick, is he? That'll bring his healer friend running. Then we'll have him!' Mary could imagine the knives being sharpened, the coil of rope being prepared for the day they could tie up the healer and take him away. It felt as if her brother's illness was the bait in a trap, waiting to snare the healer, because he was its enemy. His enemies were like a disease, waiting to lash out and grab fresh victims whenever they could.

'He's got to come, hasn't he?' she said out loud. But she wasn't sure.

Next day, there was still no word. Lazarus was now having to fight for every breath. IN . . . OUT . . . IN . . . OUT . . . Martha spent more time sitting with him, as Mary kept dissolving into floods of tears at the sight of so much pain. It wasn't right, Martha thought. It wasn't right. Why should her family be singled out for things like this to happen? Lazarus hadn't done anything wrong! It wasn't as if he'd killed or cheated anyone so you could say he deserved it. Martha was a practical soul, so she busied herself with checking her brother's temperature, taking off or putting on extra blankets if his fever took him too much one way or the other. Now and then, she tried to give him a little water to drink. She didn't know if it did any good, but you had to keep busy.*

She remembered that awful dinner party when the servants had nearly gone on strike and it was left to her and her sister to sort out the catering for the healer and his friends. What chaos that was! Dirty plates coming back to the kitchen, food ready to go out and nothing to put it on. Then Mary disappeared, and Martha had to go and drag her away from the meeting, because Mary was so taken with listening to what the healer had to say. Martha smiled. She'd sworn at Mary, and the healer had told her off for it. She smiled again at the memory. It was good to meet someone who wasn't afraid of her.

Lazarus started coughing badly, his body stiffening and turning, almost rolling off the bed. She tried holding him down, but the spasms were too strong.

'Mary! Mary!' She needed help and Mary came running into the room.

[Together, they held him down, willing him to be still, but the coughing only became worse. He seemed to be choking on something. Another bout of

coughing – then a long-drawn-out sigh. Lazarus became still. The two sisters stood back. There was no need to check if he still had a pulse. They knew.*] or

[But it was too late. Everything went quiet.]

'He's gone, Martha,' Mary whispered.

Martha nodded. It was the end. Already her mind was listing all the preparations that would have to be made, all the people who would have to be contacted. She wondered if the healer would be able to come to the funeral.

Then something in her strong organized mind snapped, and she shouted as loud as she could, 'WHERE IS HE?'

Mary looked at her, puzzled. 'In heaven, I suppose.'

'That's not who I meant! WHERE IS THE HEALER? He can make the blind see and the lame walk! Where was he when we needed him most?'*

Mary looked back at the body. 'Somewhere else, I suppose.'

'That's not good enough! He's supposed to be with us!'

'Maybe he is, in a way.' Mary looked down at her brother. 'I just know this won't be the end of it.'

Martha shrugged. Her sister didn't make sense sometimes, but it was good to have her here on a day like today. They gave each other a hug. Then, holding hands, they left the room and went to spread the news that a funeral was due to take place. They both felt incredibly alone, but at least they were alone together.*

UNIT 4

Teacher's notes

 Aim To consider the process of grieving, and the support that family members can give each other at times of crisis.

This story is an extrapolation of the first part of an episode in John 11.1-43. I have purposely not included the account of the raising of Lazarus because the 'happy ending' would detract from what is here a study of grief. You may wish to finish the unit with a straight reading from verses 17 to 44, for which some follow-up work is provided.

You will need to be sensitive to the needs of children in your class who have suffered a bereavement. This is no reason for avoiding this subject, but do be prepared for tears. Your classroom may be the first place where they've been given space to express their feeling on the subject, and a hug from one of their friends or a touch on the shoulder from you (and some clean paper handkerchiefs) will help. Allow space at the end of the lesson for children to 'wind down'. Some may want to talk to you. Be prepared. What encouraging words would you have for a bereaved child? Don't make this the last lesson of the day – give them space to settle before going home. (The 'Strong feelings' section in Appendix 1 of this book (see p. 91) may have useful ideas for you.)

It may be worth saying later that scratches or cuts rarely lead to serious illness nowadays. We now know more about germs than the people in the story did, and can prevent most infections with antibiotics.

You may wish to substitute the actual 'death scene' (indicated in the story in brackets) with the shorter, less dramatic phrase indicated immediately afterwards in brackets. Don't use both.

 Prompts A stretcher or bed for a prop! (Does the school have one in sick-bay?) A glass of water.

Reinforcement of the biblical story

1. Describe the different ways in which Mary and Martha cared for their sick brother.

(First, discuss in small groups and provide prompts on board.)

2. This story is only a small part of a much longer story. Find out what happens when the healer arrives by reading John 11.1-37. If you've been to a Christian funeral, you might have heard verse 25 read out as part

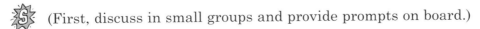

of the service. What do you think Jesus meant when he said it? Some people have thought it could mean:

● that believing in Jesus will make you his friend so he will look after you when you die;

● that one day, all the people who believe in Jesus will come back to life;

● that when you start believing in Jesus, you start living a new life now that will never end, even if your body stops working.

What do *you* think? Why do *you* think it is used at Christian funerals? Copy out that verse, with your explanation. Why did you choose that one? Can you think of some way to illustrate it?

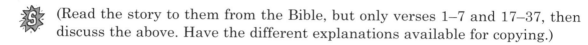 (Read the story to them from the Bible, but only verses 1–7 and 17–37, then discuss the above. Have the different explanations available for copying.)

3. To finish the story, read the episode described in John 11.38-44. Create a list of 'feelings' that are being expressed by Mary or Martha through the whole story that started at verse 1. Draw these as a series of masks, with captions to put each mask at a different place in the story.

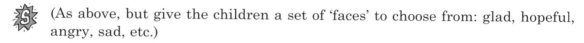 (As above, but give the children a set of 'faces' to choose from: glad, hopeful, angry, sad, etc.)

PSE

1. Have you ever been sick for a long period? Who cared for you? What helped you to feel a little better, even though you were sick? Write about it.

(As above, but get them to draw themselves in bed surrounded by the things they needed to help themselves feel better.)

2. What sorts of qualities does it take to be a carer for the sick? Write a job advert for someone who will have to care for an elderly lady on a 24-hour basis. Describe in detail what tasks the job will involve.

3. If somebody becomes very sick, or even dies, their family and friends will feel very sad about it. How did Mary and Martha show their sadness and grief? Does everybody do it in the same way? How do you show that you are sad? Write about the things that make people upset, and the ways that people show it, in an article or a poem entitled 'Feeling Sad'.

(As above, but drawing a sad face labelled 'Feeling Sad', with illustrations with captions around it. It may help others in your class if, in a small group or on a class basis, you create a word list for this activity.)

Literacy work

1.   What are the main stages of this story? Most stories have some kind of *intro-duction* (to characters and setting), then a *build-up* (of tension), then a *climax* (where the tension is turned up to its highest point), and finally a *resolution* (where the tension is eased). Read through the story again. Can you see where each stage starts and finishes? Write about how this story works, explaining what happens at each stage, and how it moves on to the next stage.

2.   The title of this story is 'The healer'. Read through the story and decide if you think this is an appropriate title. Can you think of a better one? Give a reason for your answer.

3.   Mary and Martha have different personalities, even though they are sisters. How would you describe them as people? How do they help each other? Use these and other questions to write an imaginary interview with one (or both) of the sisters, for inclusion in a local newspaper on the occasion of their brother's death. (See below for extension.)

To expand on the above, read about the dinner party that was going wrong in Luke 10.38-42. Include a memory of it in the interview.

4.   Study the poem 'A sonnet for a rabbit' (see p. 85). A sonnet is a very stylish way of writing poetry, and it has a particular shape. Can you see how it has been made to rhyme? The letters on the right-hand side are a code to show which lines are meant to rhyme with each other. Choose a subject you want to write about, and make a few notes about what you want to say – then compose your own poem. You must make it fit the rhyming scheme, and it must have fourteen lines.

5.   Read the poem 'Kiss' (see p. 86). What sort of person is speaking in the poem – can you see any clues? List that person's memories of childhood. What links them? Do you like the poem? Write about it, listing the lines that you like and dislike, and saying why.

The healer

WORKSHEET 1

Name_____ **Date**_____

Read or listen to the story, then answer the following.

1. Write three words for each woman to describe her feelings.

Mary	**Martha**
_____	_____
_____	_____
_____	_____

2. Draw one face for Mary and one for Martha to express the sort of people they were.

3. What does this tell you about the different ways that Mary and Martha reacted to the same things?

_____

_____

_____

4. How do you react when something sad happens?

_____

_____

_____

The healer

WORKSHEET 2

Name_____ **Date**_____

Read the original story in John 11.1-37. You have episode one of the story.

1. Sum up what happens in three sentences.

_____

_____

_____

_____

_____

_____

2. Now read the rest of the story in John 11.38-44.
Tell the rest of the story in two sentences, and fill
in the TV screen.

_____

_____

_____

_____

3. This passage was included in the Christian Bible for a reason.
What do you think it says about Jesus?

_____

_____

_____

UNIT 5

The battle

This story is set in the time when England was ruled by the Tudors. The king was Henry VIII, who spent a lot of time and money building up the Royal Navy to protect the country in time of war. As you'll see, things didn't quite go according to plan, especially with the newest and most modern sailing ship in his fleet, the Mary Rose. *It's also a story about one family, although you'll only meet one of them in the story.*

It was a beautiful ship. Although the dockside was crowded with sailors, soldiers and dockyard workers all frantically loading supplies and weapons on to ships, Tom still had to stop and look at the *Mary Rose*. She was massive, with her three masts stretching up to heaven, her gilded paintwork glinting in the early morning sunlight, and her new set of cannons ready to blast the King's enemies into bits.

This is what it's all about, thought Tom. This is where I belong. He hoisted his apprentice carpenter's toolbox on his back and strode up the gangplank. He was only fourteen, but already he felt like a hero.

If only the folks at home could see this, he grinned. His village was a long way away from Portsmouth, and the distance made it feel even smaller and more backward. Most of the people there couldn't even spell their names, but Tom knew all his letters and could even write a short letter in English and Latin. His father had paid for some private lessons. Tom had hated the long hours practising with quill and pen, but it made him feel superior to everyone else, especially his older brother who ran the family farm. William could hardly read at all – why was *he* in charge? It hadn't seemed right to Tom, which was why he'd left home to make his own way.*

'Mind yer backs there!' yelled a pikeman, elbowing his way past Tom. The ship was filling up with soldiers loaded down with armour and weapons. Already, archers were taking up their places on the forecastle, and some were climbing rope-ladders to reach the crow's-nests. Everybody had their pre-arranged places during a battle, and archers always looked for high points for firing down onto an enemy deck. In the distance, Tom could hear drums.

He dragged his chest down some stairs and along a dark corridor until he found the carpenter's cabin. Jeremiah, the ship's master carpenter, was already there, hammering some nails into a large square of wood.

'Look at this! I ask you!' He showed Tom. 'It's not seasoned! It's warped!'

'What's it for?'

'Covering the portholes for the cannon. The whole batch has warped! I told them not to use unseasoned wood, but would they listen to me? Oh no, I'm just the fool who has to mend their mistakes afterwards because I'm good at mending.'

'Is it important?'

Jeremiah put his hammer down. 'Only if we head far out to sea. They won't be able to close some of the portholes if the waves start rolling, that's all.'

'Will it be all right today?'

'I've told the captain, but I don't think he was listening. He said not to worry, we weren't going that far.'

'Well, he *is* the captain.'

'Have you seen our new crew?' Jeremiah had been with the ship since it was built. This would be its first taste of real action. 'Most of them have only been here a week. We've only been out three times, and I'm surprised we didn't hit something. Amateurs!'

Tom felt safe with Jeremiah. The carpenter was as old as his father, but seemed to be just that little bit more interesting. His father knew about growing fruit and vegetables and running a farm estate, but that just didn't compare with Jeremiah's knowledge of the high seas. He'd met the carpenter when he was visiting a sister in Tom's village, and Tom was so impressed with his stories about life on the ocean wave, that he'd persuaded his father to let him be apprenticed as a ship's carpenter with Jeremiah.*

Of course, it had all been a scandal. His brother William was furious. ('Who's going to help me round the farm, then?' he'd said.) His father hadn't wanted him to go, but he'd provided enough money to pay for the apprenticeship and given Tom another large sum 'for emergencies'. It was spent now, because Tom liked drinking in taverns. It made him feel more like a man – he liked buying a round for others, even if they didn't buy drinks for him. Now, everything he owned was packed away in that carpenter's chest sitting in the cabin. He was glad it was locked.*

'What do we do now?' he asked. It felt a bit odd to be sitting doing nothing as the whole ship was loading up ready for battle.

Jeremiah paused from his hammering. 'At the moment, not a lot. I can't do much with those doors until we get back to port. You and me'll be needed for emergency repairs once things hot up. For now, I'd just go round with a hammer and see if anything needs nailing down if I was you. They'll be needing a hand with the netting. Help with that.'

Tom went topside to the main deck, which was fairly heaving with soldiers. Overhead, massive nets were being stretched and pegged down, covering most of the ship. It was the latest idea for stopping enemy soldiers swinging over on ropes to land on your deck. It made him feel a little uncomfortable, but he couldn't think why, apart from having a vague sense of being enclosed, hemmed in.* He helped with some of the pegging down, and then wandered around the ship, slipping past officers and crew to watch as the gangplanks were raised and the ship was pulled out into the wind by two longboats.

With a heavy flapping, the sails were unfurled, slowly filling up, and then the ship started to move on her own. It was always a wonderful moment when the ship became like a living thing again, gently forcing her way out against the sluggish tide. There wasn't much wind, but it was enough. Spectators cheered and waved from the portside. Flags began to flutter in the breeze. Even the sun was out. It felt good to be alive.*

Other ships were waiting in a deeper channel, the *Great Harry*, the *Victory*, and even the *Ark Royal*, all with loosened sails, biding their time until the squadron was ready to move together across the Solent towards the enemy – except that something was going wrong. Tom could hear his captain swearing at his officers, and the ship wasn't slowing down but speeding up as it approached the others.

As they passed the *Great Harry*, he heard a snatched exchange of words between the two captains, during which his own captain said that he had the worst crew in the fleet and that most of them weren't obeying orders, and that they were the worst bunch of knaves he'd ever had the misfortune to command.* In the distance, Tom could see the French fleet, making their way round the Isle of Wight to attack Portsmouth. War drums sounded. It was time to go down.

His heart was pumping. He didn't feel safe and he wanted to be with Jeremiah. He wanted to be with somebody older who he could trust. B-bang! B-bang! B-bang! thudded the battle drums. Was this what it was like? Jeremiah wasn't in the cabin. What should he do? Tom thought of his home and his family. They don't even know I'm in a battle, he thought. Nobody knows. Without Jeremiah, he suddenly felt very young and very alone.*

There was a small window cut in the wall to let light in, and Tom peered out. It wasn't much of a view, but he could see the French galleys coming awfully close. He'd heard that with their oars, they could run rings around a sailing ship if the wind dropped. There were some more loud bangs, not drums this time, but cannon. Tom coughed as the stench and smoke of gunpowder wafted through the window, and the walls of the ship shook.

Then it all happened at once. He felt the ship turning, then tipping, and suddenly the only thing in his window was bright blue sky. He was thrown back. Screams and yells burst through the deck above, with the scrapings and thumps of heavy cannon sliding, and ballast shifting. Then the floor tipped further and became a wall, and the wall became a floor. What was happening?*

More yells and screams. Then a word. 'Sinking!' Sinking? He had to get out. Where? He was standing on the door to the corridor. He moved, tried to open it, but it was jammed. He looked up. The window! It was small, but so was he. He tore off any bulky clothes, his carpenter's belt, climbed up and started scrabbling through the hole. It scratched and cut, but he could do it. First the head, then one shoulder, then the other. Yes, he could do it.

Soon he was on the other side, standing on the outside wall, alone, no others in sight. The ship was heeling further. No time! He dived into the cold water, not wanting to get sucked down in the undertow.

How long did he tread water for? He didn't know. There were a few others who got out, but not many – just a few of the men who'd been up in the crow's-nests. The rest were trapped like fish in the netting, dragged down to their deaths on the cold dark seabed.

Eventually, a boat came for the survivors. Afterwards, shivering under a borrowed blanket on the *Great Harry*, Tom wondered what to do now. He couldn't feel anything. He had nothing left. Jeremiah was gone. All his stories, all his knowledge and skill with wood – drowned, in a few moments.

His life, their life, had ended, and Tom would never see him again. It was all so wrong, all so . . . unfair.*

What could he do now? His apprentice tools and what money he had left were now at the bottom of the Solent, all wasted, all lost, like Jeremiah. Tom had nothing. He could join another ship, of course. He thought about it. It was strange how clearly he was thinking. No. No more going to sea. Not now. Never again. Not after seeing what he'd seen. There was only one thing left.*

He had to go home. Back at Portsmouth, he borrowed some clothes, and set off along the road that would lead eventually back to his village. He wasn't looking forward to arriving back home, because he knew what they'd all say and they were probably right. He'd have to say sorry, it had all gone wrong. Perhaps they'd let him work back on the farm. It wouldn't be the same, but it was better than nothing. He didn't think he was worth very much now anyway.*

Unit 5

Teacher's notes

 Aim To consider what it means to 'leave home'.

 Prompts Picture or model of the *Mary Rose*, or at least a Tudor warship.

This retells part of the story of the 'Prodigal Son' (Luke 15.11-32), in a Tudor context. I've purposely left it unfinished (at an earlier point than Jesus leaves it), to give more space for you to consider the ending with your class.

Reinforcement of the story theme

1. Why did Tom want to leave home? Which of the following are the 'best fit' answers? Explain your choice.

- He wanted to feel more 'grown up'.
- He didn't like the village where he lived.
- He wanted more money.
- He didn't think his father loved him.

(As above, but orally.)

2. How did his family respond to his leaving home? What do you think they were feeling? Write a letter from one of them to a friend, explaining their thoughts.

3. Use music to illustrate the story. Choose different instruments for different moods or parts of the story, then use them to create a sound background. (You will probably need to mark a copy of the text with different kinds of symbols for the different sounds you are going to use.) Practise, then perform it as extracts of the story are read out. Don't forget to include a way of showing how Tom felt at different times. Maybe you could use the sound of a particular instrument to show this.

4. Retell the story in 'willow-pattern' style, placing all the major events on one design drawn on a paper plate, as used on the traditional willow pattern. Draw a second plate to show how the story could end.

Reinforcement of the biblical story

1. This story is retelling part of the famous tale of the 'Prodigal Son', as told by Jesus. You can find it in the Bible at Luke 15.11-32 (see

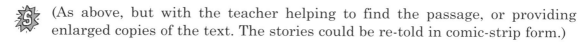

p. 108). Jesus didn't finish his story – we don't know what happened next, because it ends with the father explaining something to the elder son. How would you finish the story? Write two alternative endings, either to the story as told by Jesus, or to the version involving Tom. Make one of the endings realistically happy, and the other realistically unhappy.

(As above, but with the teacher helping to find the passage, or providing enlarged copies of the text. The stories could be re-told in comic-strip form.)

2. Compare the two stories – the one told by Jesus and the one about Tom. Which parts are the same in both stories, and which are different? (Why do you think this story is included in the Bible? Is it just a story, or does it have a deeper message?)

PSE

1. Both stories include moments when the younger son has to make decisions about his future. The decision to go back and say 'Sorry' was probably the hardest. Why? Have you ever had to say 'Sorry' in a difficult situation? Write a poem (acrostic or haiku) or a short story about being sorry.

2. Discuss, with the following prompts on the board:

'As I get older, at home I want to be able to . . .'

'As I get older, at home I will need to take responsibility for . . .'

As we grow older, we find ourselves wanting more freedom, but this also means that we have to make a greater contribution to running the family home. What things will you need to take responsibility for as you grow older? Write about 'My Future', describing the things you want to be able to do, but also writing about the responsibilities you'll be needing to take on.

(This theme is taken up in another story, 'The ration book' (see p. 47).)

Literacy work

1. The story of the 'Prodigal Son' has been told for centuries in all sorts of different ways. Find the original story as told by Jesus in Luke 15.11-31. Can you plot the main parts of the story, and number them? The author of 'The battle' placed the story in Tudor times, and added lots of detail about everyday life in Tudor times to help make it realistic. Can you retell the story by placing it in another historical period? You could even place it in the present – or the future! Remember, you *must* come up with believable settings and characters, or the reader won't care what happens to the characters in your story. You will need to give special thought to working out why the younger character left home – and why he finally returns.

2. Read the poem 'Eric the wolf cub' (see p. 83). Can you see any similarities between it and the Bible story? This is a *narrative* poem, meaning that it tells a story. Can you explain the appeal of the poem? How does it 'work'? Read it through again, and then retell it as a short *prose* story.

The battle

WORKSHEET 1

Name_____   **Date** _____

Read or listen to the story, then answer these questions.

1.   Why did Tom want to leave home? Look at the possible answers below. Which are the best ones? Tick them.

● He wanted to feel more 'grown up'.

● He didn't like the village where he lived.

● He wanted more money.

● He didn't think his father loved him.

2.   Imagine this is a letter from Tom to his dad, written when he wants to come home. Complete the letter.

Dear Dad,

I am sorry_____

_____

_____

_____

_____

_____

_____

_____

_____

_____

_____

The battle

WORKSHEET 2

Name_____ **Date** _____

Read the original story of the man with two sons in Luke 15.11-31, then answer the following:

1. Look at the pictures of the characters below. Which one do you think is the lost son, the older brother and the father? Give reasons for your answer.

_____   _____   _____
_____   _____   _____
_____   _____   _____

2. Why did the lost son go back in the original story? Read verses 17 to 20, and list some reasons.

_____
_____
_____

3. Look at the pictures of the characters again. Imagine that the father was on the left, and the older brother in the middle. What other responses could these two have made when the lost son came home?

_____
_____
_____

UNIT 6

The ration book

This story takes place during the Second World War, about 60 years ago, when our country was at war with Germany. The German leader, Adolf Hitler, decided that the best way to defeat our country was to starve us and make us too scared to carry on fighting. So he sent submarines to sink the ships that brought food to our country, and sent his air force to drop lots of bombs on our cities. Any city with a large harbour was bombed very badly, and lots of children across the country had to get used to hiding in shelters when the bombs started falling. It was a very frightening time.

'Where is it? It must be there!'

The ration book wasn't there. Susan knew it had been there on Tuesday because she'd gone to the butcher's on Tuesday, early. She'd been told that some bacon was just in, and she'd wanted to be first in the queue, even if it meant being late for school. Now it was Thursday and the book was missing – a nearly new six-month ration book with all their entitlements to meat, butter, sweets and everything else that you could only buy 'on the ration' because there was a war on, and there wasn't enough to go round. Everyone had to have a ration book. Each book had the same number of tokens for meat, butter and everything else you wanted. Her own book was the last one in the family with some meat coupons in it. Without it, her family would be without meat for weeks.* They'd be sunk.

Like her elder brother's ship. Had Edward's ship been sunk? She didn't want to think about that. There was no news, and he was usually so good at writing letters, wherever he was. The flow of letters had stopped, just like that, which could only mean that something awful had happened. She imagined Edward's ship being hit by a torpedo and sinking, and Edward clinging to a life-raft. She wanted to see him again, even though they'd fought like cats when they were growing up. Then all of a sudden it seemed he'd grown up, put on a Royal Navy uniform and joined a ship fighting submarines on the Atlantic convoys that brought all the extra things that the country needed from overseas. 'I'm off to save your bacon!' he'd joked.*

Where was her ration book? She searched the sideboard again, going through all the drawers (what was the torch doing there?), checking behind the clock and opening every magazine and newspaper to check it hadn't been folded up in there by mistake. Dad would be home soon, and there was nothing on the table. Mum's war work was all well and good, but someone still had to cook the meals and wash up, and Susan was stuck with having to do some of it.*

One day it might be just washing up. Another day it would be heating up something that Mum had left behind on the stove. Today, Susan was supposed to be cooking the whole meal. She'd missed an after-school netball practice to come home, take the money stuffed under the clock and go out to buy some corned beef – but that was impossible without the book. It wasn't where they'd normally left it, behind the clock. What should she do now?

She sat staring at the clock. Her father would be in soon, wanting his tea. She pouted. It wasn't her fault! Other girls in her class didn't have to do this. Their mums stayed at home to do the housekeeping. Why did it have to be *her* mum who had to go out and make artillery shells at the factory? It wasn't fair. She'd get all the blame, and she knew it. And that is exactly what happened.

'No tea, y'say? I don't believe it! I've been slaving away down the docks all day, I'm on emergency air-raid duty in an hour and you've got nothing on for tea?' He stamped up the stairs in a huff to get changed. 'Where did you leave the book, then?' he shouted down as he took his big steel-capped boots off. She told him, and said it wasn't there now. 'For pity's sake! It's the most important book you've got in the whole blasted house and you have to lose it! Is there anything else in the larder?'

There was only some bread, margarine and a piece of whalemeat that even the cat wouldn't eat. 'A sandwich? Is that it? Not even a piece of cheese?' He looked in all the places she'd looked already, and then sat down with the sandwich, grumbling as she made him a cup of tea.*

It wasn't fair, she thought, as she poured herself a cup as well. Nothing's fair. The rationing's unfair and my family's unfair, and it's all because of a little book. For lack of anything else to do, she pulled out her knitting and did a few rows. She was hungry, but decided not to do anything about it until her father had gone off on duty. Mum would be in by then, and she could sort something out for them both by borrowing off a neighbour. She'd understand. Susan didn't feel very understood.*

Nobody had talked about her brother's ship possibly sinking once the letters had stopped, in case talking about it made things worse. Instead, they all thought about it by themselves. She knew that, from the way everyone was tense if there was an unexpected knock on the front door, just in case it was a message-boy bringing the dreaded telegram that would say that her brother was 'lost at sea'. You only ever saw a message-boy in their neighbourhood if he was bringing bad news. No one seemed to be able to talk about it, so they were just getting on with their lives. She'd been knitting this scarf for Edward. NO! She *was* knitting it for him, and she *would* give it to him when he came back. Edward would come back. She knew it, and by knowing it she thought she could make it happen.*

The sirens started wailing just before six o'clock, making great whooping noises that gave you goose bumps as you frantically thought of all the things you had to do. Were the blackouts up? Dad had already gone, giving her a kiss on the forehead as always but not looking her in the eyes. She was alone in the house, waiting for her mum to come home, but it looked as if Hitler and his bombs were getting here first. Should she go to one of the neighbours? She didn't know. Mum would be frightened to come home to an empty house. Should she leave a note?*

There was a dull thud in the distance, and then another. Bombs. Too late! She ran upstairs, grabbed a blanket and her gasmask, and raced out to the shelter at the bottom of the garden. It wasn't much of a shelter, really. They'd been too late to buy an Anderson, so Dad had gone for the next best thing: an old car rescued from a scrapyard and buried in a great hole in the garden under some railway sleepers and packed earth. She scrabbled down the ladder into the hole, dodged the puddle at the bottom, opened the driver's door and slipped in. There was no steering wheel – the inside had been stripped so that the whole family could hide here during an air raid. She fumbled in the glove compartment for a torch, found it was missing, then gazed in puzzlement at the little book she'd found instead. She remembered, and relaxed. Too late now.*

Already she could hear the drone drone droning of the bombers heading for the docks that were only a few streets away. The forgotten sirens were still wailing. Already she knew that the searchlights would be stroking the clouds with their long thin fingers, trying to find an enemy plane for our own guns to aim at. Thump. Another bomb, nearer. Thump, like a giant's footstep slamming onto hard ground. She imagined a giant Hitler stamping on people's houses, his great jackboots coming ever closer. There was a crackle of anti-aircraft fire. Thump. Another footprint, shaking the ground.

Please God, get me out of this. Thump. I'll never moan again. I'll be really good. Thump, a street away. I'll be good. Look after me. Our Father which art in heaven. THUMP. Hallowed be thy name. Thy Kingdom come. THUM-MMP! The whole car shook. Something hammered down on the car roof, bending it, pushing it down almost onto her head. 'DADDY!' Susan screamed. She fiddled with the car door handle, but the whole door was buckled and it wouldn't open. The driver's window had smashed. She scrabbled in the dark to take off her shoe and started knocking out bits of broken glass with the heel so she could climb out without hurting herself. THUMMP! The giant was filling in the hole by kicking in bits of brick and earth, filling it up so she couldn't escape. She was trapped.

Sit still. Don't panic. That's what her dad had said, and he should know because he was an Air-raid Warden. If a bomb hits you and you're still alive, then don't panic. Try to get out before something else falls on you. She felt to her right. Loose earth had poured in through the broken window – the sides of the shelter must have collapsed. She started digging, scooping it out with her nails and fingers, first feeling carefully for broken glass and then not bothering. It can't be that far. The soil was in her face, in her hair, in her eyes. Don't panic, her dad had said. He'd dug out enough people from fallen buildings. What had happened to the house? She kept digging until a hand found fresh air. Half crawling, she reached through, widening the hole, and then squeezed her way through the window, out and up through the loose earth, coughing as dirt went down her throat.*

She was outside, but the garden had vanished, covered with massive lumps of masonry and roof tiles. The house must have suffered a direct hit. She heard someone crying, then realized it was her own voice, sobbing. Her clothes, face and hair were covered in mud; her knees and arms were scratched and bleeding. She was all alone. Nobody knew she was here – that her home had been blown to bits, and she was bleeding.

Thump. Another footprint. Thump, louder. The giant was coming closer to get her. She could hear him whistling. She stood there, frozen stiff, waiting to be broken like a matchstick doll.*

'Susan! This way!' There was a voice from the house, a voice she knew.

'Susan! Run! This way!' She turned towards the voice, then stumbled towards it through the rubble, clambering through the broken walls and timbers of her home. She tripped over, banged her head, then was swept up by two powerful arms that lifted her out, over a wall and out onto the street. Someone shouted at everybody to get down.

Then the giant stamped on them. BOOOOM! Roaring with delight, he blasted the breath out of their lungs as his jack-boot heel ground them into the dust. Then it all seemed to go quiet.

After a while, Susan moved. There was a weight on her, the weight of some-one's body. She shifted a little, and the weight moved, too. She turned her head to see. It was her dad, wearing his black helmet with 'ARP' on it in big white painted letters. There was blood on his face, but he was smiling at her. He'd covered her with his own body to shield her from the blast. Slowly, painfully, he climbed off then knelt by her side, gently wiping the dust from her face with a handkerchief.

'All right, pet?' She saw the smile, nodded, smiled back then closed her eyes. She'd done as she'd been told. Then there was a thought at the back of her memory that opened her eyes wide.

'I've found it!' she said.

'You've found what, pet?'

'The ration book!'

'Oh that! Well . . . er . . . well done!'

She felt better now as she closed her eyes. Her dad had come back for her – and they were both safe.*

UNIT 6

Teacher's notes

Aim To look at the parent/child relationship in terms of authority and obedience, and love and understanding, using ideas contained in Paul's letter to the Ephesians 6.1-4.

Prompts Pictures associated with the Home Front during the Second World War, especially air-raid precautions. A picture of Adolf Hitler.

One of the related poems, 'Albert and the roller coaster' (see p. 88), is based on another much more famous poem – 'The lion and Albert', by Marriot Edgar, found in many anthologies. It will be worth obtaining a copy so that children can compare the two for literacy development.

Reinforcement of the story and biblical theme

1. List the different responsibilities that Susan and her parents faced.

(As above, but orally, then drawn and labelled as 'Susan's jobs' etc.)

2. What would the consequences have been for her parents if Susan had chosen to do nothing to help around the house? Write about how their lives would have been different.

3. 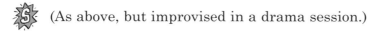 Look at the passage in Paul's letter to the Ephesians 6.1-4 (see p. 109). Create the script for a short play that illustrates both halves of the same quote. Possible scenarios could include 'Bedtime', 'Tidy your room' or 'Turn that stereo down'.

(As above, but improvised in a drama session.)

PSE

1. Create a cartoon showing modern parents and children with the following caption: 'You treat this place like a hotel, and us like servants!' Think about why the parents feel that way. What are the children *not* doing?

(Give prompts for possible situations, especially a very untidy child's bedroom.)

2. What can children give to their parents, not in 'things', but in 'doing'? Give some examples.

Literacy work

1.   Study the part of the story that relates to the air raid. It's all written from Susan's viewpoint. List the words and phrases that help to give you a 'feel' of what it was like to be there. At one point, Susan feels that she is being chased by some kind of giant. Why?

2.   A lot of stories use a kind of picture language for feelings. Dragons, giants and other monsters appear in lots of stories, and somebody usually has to end up fighting them. The author Terry Pratchett once said that children need to read stories about monsters, because they need to know that nasty things can be beaten. What do *you* think? Should stories carry a message? Draft and write a monster story for a younger person that encourages them to be brave in some way. Include lots of exciting description!

3.   Read the poem 'Discontented murmurs' (see p. 87). In a small group, assign parts to everybody, then plan a dramatic performance with expression and appropriate gestures, marking your script to show which words need expression and emphasis.

4.   Read the poem 'Albert and the roller coaster' (see p. 88). This is based on another famous poem called 'The lion and Albert'. Read this, too, and compare them. Can you see any similarities? Look for particular phrases and characters, and the way that the poem is organized in verses. Which poem do you prefer? Why? Write about it, listing events, phrases or lines in either poem that you like or dislike.

The ration book

WORKSHEET 1

Name_____ **Date**_____

Listen to or read the story, then answer the following.

1. List the different responsibilities that Susan faced.

    _____
    _____
    _____

2. List the responsibilities that her parents faced.

    _____
    _____
    _____

3. What would have happened if Susan had chosen to do nothing to help around the house?

    _____
    _____
    _____

4. What would have happened if her parents had chosen to do nothing to help out at home, or hadn't bothered to go out to work?

    _____
    _____
    _____
    _____

The ration book

WORKSHEET 2

Name_____ **Date**_____

Read some advice about family life in Ephesians 6.1-4.

It gives two pieces of advice which need to be balanced. Write on the pan scales the advice to parents, and the advice to children. Draw an illustration for each piece of advice nearby.

Do you think this advice would help people today? How? Why?

_____

_____

_____

_____

_____

UNIT 7

The quiver of arrows

This is a story about life in a Victorian school, about 120 years ago. In those days, schools were run in a very different way. See what you think. It's also about the way boys and girls are sometimes treated differently.

The day started like any other day in the Board School, with a story, a hymn and a prayer, and then the children sat down to their lessons. As a monitor, Sarah's first job was to ensure that all the children in her class, class III, had a clean slate and a sharp piece of chalk to practise their numbers and letters, copying from the wall where they had been painted last summer. Miss Prissick had painted the letters and numbers herself, being a strong believer in young children learning them early.

Once the class were started, Sarah went back to her teacher to be given her own lesson, in arithmetic, with the other class monitors. Miss Prissick explained again how to multiply the large numbers, then wrote some problems up on the blackboard.

'Let's see which of you can finish them first. Off you go!'

The monitors raced off to their own desks at the end of each row, placed so they could keep an eye on their own classes while doing their own work. Miss Prissick was meanwhile filling in the register at the front. Altogether, there were about 80 children in the school hall, taught by one schoolmistress and her twelve monitors. The monitors were really her top class – boys and girls aged between eleven and twelve. Besides learning their own lessons, they had to teach the younger ones. It was hard work, but they were paid a half-penny every week for doing it – and for some, that was better than going to work at the factory.*

Sarah found it hard to concentrate. Alfie, at the other end of her row, was trying to poke the girl in front with his pencil. He was only eight, and was bored with copying. Sarah went along the line.

'Alfie! Stop it! Get on with your letters!'

'I'm bored, Sarah.' He meant it.

'You'll be in trouble if you don't!' She pointed at Miss Prissick, who was looking in their direction. 'I'll tell!'

Alfie knew where that would lead, and went back to his slate. When Sarah said something, she meant it. He didn't like girls, but she was bigger than him and in charge, and his mum said he had to do as he was told in school 'If he was going to be learned proper', as she put it. He knew he could leave school when he was about eleven, and couldn't wait.*

Back at her desk, Sarah couldn't concentrate on the arithmetic. She was wondering how the new baby was. The nurse had come to the house late last night, and Sarah had heard a lot of yelling. She didn't know that her mum knew such words, and they came out awfully loud and fast. The nurse had sent them all out – her father, her brothers and sisters and herself, and they'd all had to wait downstairs, listening to the strange sounds. Being eldest, Sarah had taken over looking after the others that night, telling them stories and getting them singing songs while her father stared vacantly out of the window at the new gaslamp in the street. Then, round about 10 o'clock, her new brother 'arrived'. The nurse came down to invite everybody up, and they all crowded round the bedside to see him asleep in his mother's arms, a tiny little lump of red wrinkles breathing softly. Her poor mum looked exhausted.*

'That's all now,' said Father. 'Time for bed.' He was smiling as they all kissed goodnight and left. Another boy. She could tell her dad was pleased.

Sarah didn't mind it being another boy. She was quite sure of that. She already had two younger brothers and a sister, not counting the ones who'd died early. Her parents seemed to treat them all fairly, and she was trusted with a lot because she was eldest – doing some of the family shopping, helping with the sewing and what have you, but it didn't seem fair. You wouldn't find many boys helping with the shopping and sewing.

The boys seemed to have it easier. They would be paid more when they were older, and they were allowed to do more interesting jobs. They were allowed to go out and play rough games. She didn't want to play football in the playground, but it would be nice to be asked. Boys would have a job like her dad, and she would have to be either a mother or an old maid, but neither seemed to be particularly exciting. She wanted to be a mother, of course, but already she could read and write better than her own mother, and felt it ought to be worth something.*

Some of the other monitors had finished their arithmetic, and she was only halfway through, even though it was easy. She decided to concentrate, still keeping a watchful eye on Alfie.

Then it was Scripture. Each class had to copy out a small portion of the Bible, the older ones using pen and ink. Sarah had already filled her tray of inkwells and took them along the line, giving Alfie a particularly hard stare that said she knew exactly what he wanted to do with his pen to the girl in front, and he wasn't going to do it here.

The class had little copybooks for Scripture, and the portion to be copied was found in a little book that was given to each child, donated by the Society for Promoting Christian Knowledge. Today's was a passage from the Psalms:

> Children are a gift from the LORD;
> they are a real blessing.
> The sons a man has when he is young
> are like arrows in a soldier's hand.
> Happy is the man whose quiver is full of them. (Psalm 127)

Boys again! Doesn't anyone want to have girls? She imagined a quiver of arrows, only with a load of silly boys' heads sticking out of the top. All of a sudden, her head filled with a question and she wanted to ask someone about it.* She got up and went to Miss Prissick's desk. The schoolmistress was noting something down in a large ledger, but looked up with a smile.

'Yes, Sarah?'

'Miss, it's this passage.' She showed it. 'Doesn't it say anything about girls as well?'

Miss Prissick looked slightly puzzled. 'What do you mean?'

'I mean . . . sorry miss, I'm not trying to be rude or anything, but what's wrong with having daughters as well?'

Miss Prissick read it, then sighed. Sarah felt it wasn't a new question to her.

'Well . . . nothing, really, Sarah.'

'Well, is there another bit that talks about how good it is to have girls?'

Miss Prissick thought for a minute through all the Sunday sermons she'd listened to at the chapel, then sighed again. 'I can't think of anything quite like that passage. They just thought about boys and girls differently in those days.'

'It's just the same now, isn't it?'*

There was a queue of children building up. Miss Prissick was starting to look flustered.

'Let me find you another passage.' She pulled out a school Bible and flicked through it. 'Here! Proverbs 31 – the Good Wife.' Sarah went back, clutching the big black book and ignored Alfie, who was under his desk and picking his nose. The new passage talked about a woman who sounded quite strong and clever. It wasn't about daughters, but at least it made a girl sound as if she could be important some day. She copied parts of it and drew what she thought a ruby looked like, since it said that a good wife was finer than rubies. For the rest of the day, she felt that Miss Prissick was treating her in a more grown-up way, as if something had changed.

That evening, after doing the family shopping, she talked about it with her mother, who was feeling a little better and was just thinking of getting up.

Why were boys thought to be more important than girls?

'They don't have to be, pet,' her mother answered, giving her a hug. 'It's what you are that counts, not what other people think about you.* Now wait here. We've got some news.' She shouted downstairs. 'Eric! Could you come upstairs, and bring that letter with you?'

Her father brought up a letter, which had already been opened. He motioned the others to sit down, then slowly and carefully read it aloud.

'"Dear Mr Anderton . . ." That's me!' he grinned. (He didn't normally receive many letters.) '"For the last six years, your daughter Sarah has shown diligence and ability in her education, and has in the last year performed an excellent service as class monitor. The Hartlepool School Board has lately made available some money for the appointment of a Pupil Teacher, to begin in September, at a starting annual remuneration of five pounds." Five pounds?' he remarked. 'That's not bad for an apprenticeship. I'll go on, "Would you please consider encouraging your daughter to apply for the post as soon as she reaches her thirteenth birthday, as I am sure she has the makings of an excellent teacher. On her sixteenth birthday, she would then be able to attend a training college, for which a grant would be made available. I look forward to discussing this with you further at a future date. Yours sincerely, signed Miss Alexandra Prissick."'

The room was silent. Then Sarah spoke. 'Alexandra? I didn't know she was called Alexandra.'

Then her mother started laughing, and then her father, and then she did too, and the rest of the family came running up to see what all the fuss was about. The baby started crying too, but nobody minded. Sarah wasn't even thirteen years old and she now had prospects!* Then she had a thought.

'Dad?'

'What?'

'Do you know what a quiver is?'*

UNIT 7

Teacher's notes

 Aim To consider the different roles in society and the home assigned to boys and girls, and other forms of 'pressure'. The biblical theme is based on Paul's comment in Romans 12.2, and the ideas expressed in Psalm 127 and Proverbs 31.10-31.

 Prompts Pictures and artefacts from a Victorian schoolroom.

This story uses a Victorian setting to consider how girls are treated, but the subject could be opened up to consider any form of stereotyping or pressure placed on children by wider society. Please stress that some of the pressures placed on children (and adults) are for their own benefit, right down to 'eating your greens' – but part of 'growing up' includes a developing ability to choose the 'right path' for oneself. For Christians and others, this involves finding God's will for one's life.

You may find it useful to have research materials available on Victorian life, and some modern magazines that you can cut up for a display.

Reinforcement of the story theme and PSE

1. Pick a scene from the story, pausing it like you can pause a video. Who are the people in the picture? What are they thinking or saying? Draw and explain the scene with captions.

 (Direct pupils to working on the final scene, discussing first what all the characters will be thinking.)

2. 'It's what you are that counts, not what other people think about you.' Do you agree? Can you think of ways in which boys and girls are treated differently today? Do you think it's right? What would you change? Can you think of any other ways in which people are judged not by what sort of person they are, but by something else? Write what you think about it.

3. Do films, television and advertising pressure you to look or behave in a different way? How? Collect pictures from magazines to create a small display of 'pressures'. Labels could include 'This suggests that all boys/girls are . . .'

4. Start a class 'chat-room', like they have on the Internet. Write your thoughts clearly on a piece of paper and stick them on a noticeboard, then see who replies. Ask other people to add their (signed) opinions underneath.

Possible topics:

- Why girls shouldn't be allowed to play football.'

- A woman's place is in the home!'

- 'Boys mess about because they're not as clever as girls.'

Reinforcement of the biblical theme

1. Read Paul's words in Romans 12.2. It's about resisting the bad things that people want you to do. Discuss bad influences (e.g. a friend who wants you to steal something) and good influences (e.g. people who want you to do well at school). Draw yourself with the good and bad influences on your left and right. Try to make the good influences look more interesting than the bad!

(In discussion, create a list of possible situations where children feel pressured, and make suggestions for layout, possibly involving faces and speech bubbles.)

2. Find the Bible passage about the Good Wife referred to in Proverbs 31.10-31. It's a picture of an ideal woman who is very important and clever and wise. Use it to create an illustrated advertisement for a wife: 'Wanted! . . .'

Then create one for a husband as well! (Will it be similar in some ways?)

Literacy work

1. Sarah's job as a monitor is very different from the sorts of tasks a child would be expected to perform in a modern school. Study the opening part of the story for clues about what school life was like in Victorian times. (Are there any things that surprise you?) Use this to write a report about some of the differences between your classroom and a Victorian one. (Which do you prefer? Why?)

(Some children will be helped if they have access to illustrations of Victorian classrooms, either for the stimulus, or so that they can label or annotate the illustrations.)

2. School life has changed a great deal over the years, and considerable thought now goes into working out how children can learn well. How did *you* learn to read and write? Are there any teachers or other people who managed to help you? How did they do it? What do you think are the best ways to help somebody to learn how to read and write? What sorts of things do you think children should be writing about? Plan, draft and write a piece entitled 'How children learn to read and write', to explain how you think it all works – and use lots of examples from your own experiences to back up what you say.

3. In Victorian times, men and women (and boys and girls) often led very different lives. Analyse the story for clues about this and describe them. Research other differences between the sexes in Victorian times and compile a report about them.

The quiver of arrows

WORKSHEET 1

Name_____ **Date**_____

1.   Listen to or read the story.

This is the final scene from the story, where Sarah's father reads the letter. What is he saying and thinking? What about Sarah herself, and her mother? Add thought and speech bubbles to show what's going on.

2.   Before she was offered the job of Pupil Teacher, Sarah was angry at not being offered the same chances as the boys. List some of the things that she was cross about.

_____

_____

_____

3.   Do you think she was right? Why?

_____

_____

_____

The quiver of arrows

WORKSHEET 2

Name_____ **Date**_____

1. What sorts of things do different people want you to do at home and at school? Draw yourself here, with the things that different people want you to do. Put a circle around one thing that you think is good and say why. Put a cross by one thing you think is not so good and say why.

2. Find and read Romans 12.2, and copy it here.

_____

_____

_____

3. Christians ask God to change the way they think. This helps them to stand up to all the bad pressures. What things help *you* to say 'no' when you are being asked to do something that you know is wrong?

_____

_____

_____

UNIT 8
Homework

'Get out! GET OUT!' Mark was shoved out of the front door and sent off to school. He could still hear his mum shouting inside, this time at his little sister. The day had started rather badly.

He'd woken as normal at 7.00, gone for a cuddle with Mum and Dad in their bedroom and then gone off to get dressed. It was while his first sock was being pulled on that he noticed the *Star Wars* X-wing fighter that was a special present from his grandfather, so it seemed a good time to take it for a few spins around his bedroom before attacking the Death Star. Then he assembled a strong force of rebels to lead a major assault on the jungle planet that was situated under his bed. This was why his mum called him at 7.30, still with one sock on and mumbling about trusting the Force.

'Mark! Aren't you ready yet? We're having breakfast! Come on down now!'*

'I'm nearly ready!'

'No you're not! You've hardly started! Get a move on!'

He pulled on the socks, climbed out of his pyjamas and was just pulling on his shirt when he saw that Luke Skywalker was in danger of falling to his death from his workdesk. Mark quickly rescued him, and then set up the next part of the adventure. This was where his dad found him at 7.50. Dad had showered, dressed, finished his breakfast, washed up and emptied the bins since rising at 7.00, and was just going to catch his train when Mum had sent him up to find Mark, who still wasn't wearing any trousers.

'Mark! Get dressed *now*!'*

Dad spoke quietly but firmly, a bit like Obi-wan Kenobi. His son did as he was told. 'Why does he have to stay and watch me? It's not fair!' he thought as he put the tie on. 'I can do it by myself!' Dad kissed him goodbye and left at 8.00.

Once downstairs, Mark nibbled some toast, then poured some milk and cereal. He was just taking the bowl towards the microwave oven when Mum asked what he was doing.

'Heating up my cereal.'

'We haven't got time for that! Go back and eat it quickly!'

'But I never have cold cereal!'

'Yes you do, and you're having it today! You've spent ages getting ready this morning and we haven't got the time! Sit down!'

It just wasn't fair. Grown-ups always bossed you around. Why couldn't they leave him alone?*

At 8.20, he was still eating his cereal when his mum came back from having her shower. 'Aren't you finished yet? Eat it NOW!' She watched closely as the last three mouthfuls disappeared, then followed him to the bottom of the stairs.

'Mark! Have you finished your homework? You've had a week to do it – it's got to be in today!'

Halfway up, he turned around, shocked. 'Today?' His mum went all quiet, then all loud.

'UPSTAIRS NOW! TEETH AND FACE AND HAIR!' He disappeared upstairs. Luke Skywalker's mum wouldn't talk to him like that, he thought, as he scrubbed his teeth. Luke Skywalker's mum would be asking if he was all right with his homework, and was there anything she could do to help.* Finished, he dashed out and went to get his school bag. It wasn't there.

It should have been at the bottom of the stairs, ready to go, but it wasn't. He looked again. Nothing.

'What's wrong?' asked Mum. She had that look in her eyes.

'I can't find my school bag!'

'Where was it?'

'Here!'

She glanced at the entrance hall clock that said 8.40. 'Well you'd better go and look for it in your room, quickly!' Mark started walking upstairs again. 'I SAID QUICKLY!' He ran. The school bag wasn't in his bedroom, although it was a bit hard to see – it would have taken a squad of Imperial Stormtroopers about a week to tidy it. No, he couldn't see it anywhere. Perhaps he'd left it in the lounge. He ran downstairs as Mum came up to go to the bathroom.

'Have you found it yet?' she puffed.

'Nearly!'

'NEARLY? HOW CAN IT BE NEARLY?'

The bag wasn't in the lounge, or under the sofa, or under the dining-room table where he'd found it yesterday after a 20-minute search. It had vanished. There was a yell from upstairs, and he went to see what was happening in the bathroom. He soon wished he hadn't. Mum was coming down the stairs, ready to explode.

'MARK! YOU'VE LEFT THE TAP RUNNING! THE SINK'S OVERFLOWED ALL OVER THE CARPET! GET YOUR SCHOOL BAG AND GO TO SCHOOL!'

'But I can't find it!'

'GET OUTSIDE NOW!'

. . . which was how he came to be outside his house in full school uniform, without his bag. What should he do now? Go to school?*

There was a click at the door and his little sister came out, ready to go to school. In her hands was Mark's school bag.

'It was under your bed!' she whispered, although no-one else was listening.*

Mark started telling his friends about it at morning break. They were mortified. How could a mum treat a child like that? It wasn't right! He started to feel like a hero, but by lunchtime, it wasn't so much fun. Some of his friends were starting to call his mum and dad names.*

By hometime, he was feeling rather upset. He could hear whispering as he walked through the small crowd. Then he heard a friendly voice.

'Mark . . . come over here.' It was Rebecca, another mum who knew his mum, whose children played with him sometimes. 'Did you have a bad morning?' He nodded tearfully. She took out her mobile phone, pressed a few numbers and then spoke into it. There was a silence, and then she looked down at Mark again.

'I've explained to your mum what's been happening today, and I've just asked if you can come back to our place for tea. She says yes. Would you like to speak to her?'*

He did, and over the phone he said sorry about the school bag and the homework. His mum sounded a lot quieter now and a bit worried. He wanted to give her a hug, but couldn't. 'Save it up for later, dear,' said Rebecca, giving him a hug. 'We all have bad mornings sometimes. Try and learn something from it. Your mum does love you, you know.' He nodded. He'd known that all the time, but he'd forgotten.*

UNIT 8

Teacher's notes

Aim   To consider practical ways of showing love, in the light of 1 Corinthians 13.

Prompts   A child's school bag, a *Star Wars* figure from the story, an alarm clock or a large clockface with hands to show the time. Keep adjusting this as the story progresses – or ask a child who can tell the time to do it!

You may wish to substitute the *Star Wars* names and phrases with others from whatever TV series or film is currently in the minds of your pupils – but plan it first and adjust your script accordingly *before* you start telling the story!

This story is a meditation on love – and how we manage not to be loving despite our best intentions. It's also about 'making up afterwards'.

Reinforcement of the story theme and PSE

1. List all the things that Mark was responsible for doing that morning. Mornings can be very busy during a normal school week. What's your morning timetable before setting off to school? What things do you have to get done that no one else can do?

 (As above, but drawn as diagrams labelled 'Mark's morning jobs' and 'My morning jobs'.)

2. List the things that Mark's mum was thinking about. How did she show she was cross? Do you think she was right to be cross? Why? What different things was Mark thinking about? Draw them both, with thought bubbles showing what Mum and Mark are thinking at the end of the morning.

3. What does being 'patient' mean to you? Write down your own definition, then look the word up in a dictionary. Are they different? How? Does being 'patient' mean that you should just put up with things that are wrong? Write about the times when you think it is right and wrong to be patient.

Reinforcement of the biblical theme

1. Read Paul's famous words about love in the Bible at 1 Corinthians 13.4-8a (see p. 110). How many descriptions of love does Paul include? Choose one that might have helped Mark or his mother to cope with the situation, and say why you have chosen it.

(As above, but they'll need support to find the passage from Paul. Otherwise give them a copy of the text, enlarged.)

2. What went wrong when Mark started discussing what happened that morning, at school? Look at verse 6 in the passage from 1 Corinthians. Can you think of any ways in which Mark's friends could have made the situation better instead of making it worse? How can friends help when we are upset about things at home? Write about it under the heading 'A friend in need'.

Literacy work

1.   There are two main points of view in this story – that of Mark, and that of his mother. Each time something happens, Mark and his mother see it in very different ways – which leads to trouble in the end. Find the 'flashpoints' in the story where he thinks about something in one way and she thinks about it in a different way, and describe the differences. (You could create an imaginary cutaway drawing of their house, and show in which places and in which order the 'flashpoints' occur.)

2.   Read the poem 'The joy of mealtimes together' (see p. 86). It's based on the different things that parents say to their young children. Everybody has a collection of 'pet' phrases that they use from time to time. What are your 'pet' phrases? Are there any you hear being used at home? Create your own free verse (non-rhyming) poem out of the things that you hear people say at home or at school.

3.   Read the poem 'The monster' (see p. 85). Each line has four words that help to keep the beat going, called 'feet'. Find and mark them on a copy of the poem, then list them. How does the 'metre' (or beat) help this poem to work? Pick a scene from the poem and illustrate it. Use some of your listed words as part of the illustration.

Homework

WORKSHEET 1

Name_____   **Date**_____

1. List three of the things that Mark was responsible for doing that morning.

    _____
    _____
    _____

2. Mornings can be very busy during a normal school week. What's your morning timetable before setting off to school? What things do you have to get done that no one else can do?

    _____
    _____
    _____

3. List some of the things that Mark's mum was having to think about.

    _____
    _____
    _____

4. How did she show she was cross? Do you think she was right to be cross? Why? What different things was Mark thinking about? Draw Mum and Mark below, with thought bubbles showing what they are thinking.

Homework

WORKSHEET 2

Name_____ **Date**_____

Read the words of Paul in 1 Corinthians 13.4-7.

1. In each of the bubbles, write one thing that Paul said about love.

2. I think Mark would have had a better morning if he had remembered to

_____

(Use one of Paul's ideas to finish the sentence.)

3. I think Mark's mum would have had a better morning if she had remembered to

_____

(Use one of Paul's ideas to finish the sentence.)

4. Which do you think is the most important of the things that Paul said about love? Why?

_____

_____

_____

UNIT 9

On the beach

In your mind, picture a beach. It's a muddy, rocky beach, with lots of pebbles, but hardly any sand. The beach stretches for miles. There are no trees. Around you, there's a strong smell, the aroma of salt. If you were to taste the water, it would be more salty than any seawater you've ever tasted before. The mineral salts are washed down from the northern mountains in the waters of the River Jordan, then left behind when the waters evaporate under the hot sun. Every year, the Dead Sea becomes more salty, as there is nowhere for the salt to go. There are no fish. Nothing can live there.

Look closer at the beach. Stretching behind it, all along the coastline, you can see a long winding track. That's the coast road. Now and then you will see people travelling on donkeys, camels or, if they're rich, on horses. Most of the people you see will be walking. There aren't many.

Today, if you look closer, you can spot three people. Go closer. They're women, one of them older, maybe in her fifties. The two others are younger, in their late teens or early twenties. They've been walking a long time and they could do with a rest. Let's go closer, and listen. The older one's just pointed to a place on the beach.

'Let's rest over there.'

She leads the way down to a spot that's hidden from the road. The others follow without comment. Each unties herself from the baggage she is carrying, then flops on the ground. They are silent for a time, taking in the view. Before them stretches the Dead Sea.

'I've heard the water's good for the feet.' That's Ruth talking. She's the youngest. 'I think I'll have a paddle.' She unties her sandals, hitches up her robe, and carefully tiptoes over the thick mud to the clearer water. The mud oozes over her toes but she doesn't mind. It's a nice change after all those miles of walking on a hard road. The water is wonderfully cool and she wiggles her toes. She looks back at the others. 'Come on! It's lovely!'

'In a bit.' That's Orpah talking. She's slightly older than Ruth. Then the other one, the older woman, speaks. That's Naomi.

'I don't know how she does it.'

Orpah turns. 'Pardon?'

'I mean, I don't know how she does it. Where does she get her energy from?'

Orpah smiles. 'It must be the water.' She gets to her feet. 'Come on! I've heard the mud makes you look ten years younger!'

Naomi shakes her head. 'Ten? I need something that'll take off a hundred years! Go on! Away with you!' she chuckles.

Orpah goes out to join Ruth, paddling. Naomi watches. She's glancing around, thinking, frowning, always weighing things up.

Someone could see them from the road. But she relaxes again. Nothing bad has happened so far, has it? After all, those men at the inn last night didn't mean any harm. They were just drunk. Still . . . She looks behind her, thinks for a moment, then gets to her feet.

Where can she . . .? Yes, there! Naomi finds a large flat rock, a good place to sit and keep a watch on the road. You can't be too careful. Women travelling without men have to be careful these days. Instinctively, she feels for the knife that she always keeps in her belt, and thanks God that she's never had to use it.

The road is deserted. She relaxes, taking a sip from her half-empty water bottle. They'll need more fresh water soon, but the River Jordan isn't that far, just one day's travel, and they can fill up again there.

She wonders about the journey. What will it be like after they've crossed the Jordan into Judaea? What will it be like in Bethlehem? She shrugs. It'll be hard, just like it's always been hard. They'll probably have to work or beg for food. The old house will still be there, but there'll be nothing in it. But there will be food. That's what she's heard. If you can work, then you'll be fed.

There are laws in Bethlehem about looking after the poor. Anything's better than staying and starving in Moab.

There's the sound of giggles and screams behind her. Naomi turns. Ruth and Orpah are having a water fight. Naomi smiles again. They're good girls. They didn't need to come with her. They could have stayed in Moab, found someone else to marry and made a new start. They didn't need to make this journey. I might be their mother-in-law, but my sons are dead now. Naomi remembers her sons and her husband, all killed when the bandits raided the town. Life wasn't fair sometimes. The neighbours had tried to help of course, but three women running a farm is hard – and when there's no rain for years, it's impossible.

Life ought to be better in Bethlehem, she thinks. She remembers playing in the streets as a child, the fruit trees full of apples and oranges, the market place full of fresh produce. She'd left it all to get married and travel. Now she's coming back with almost nothing. It's not fair on the girls, she thinks. It's not fair. They don't need to share my life if it's always going to be like this. They could make a new start.

The girls are coming back now, trying to come up the beach without getting muddy, and it isn't working. 'Yuck!' says Ruth.

'It's good for your skin!' says Orpah.

They seem cheerful enough, almost like little girls again, never mind all the sadness they've seen.

They all sit down together, unpack some food and eat. It isn't much, but it cost a lot of money in the last town they came through. They eat slowly, chewing every mouthful lots of times so they can enjoy the taste for as long as possible, and to enjoy the memory of it when they're next feeling hungry. They eat silently, concentrating on the flavour of the roasted chicken and the hard crusty bread.

When they finish, Naomi speaks. 'Girls. I've got something to say and I want you to listen. I want you to listen to all of it before you say anything. What's happened has happened. Years ago, I came here looking for a new life with a new husband, and life was good. I had two wonderful sons – and when they married you I gained two wonderful daughters. Ruth! Stop looking like that! I mean it! I loved it when you first started calling me mother. Now . . .'

Naomi looks out to sea. She gazes out over the sterile waves of the Dead Sea where nothing lives, where nothing can ever live.

'Now it's time for you to live your own lives again. No! Don't say anything yet – hear me out, Orpah! You've seen me almost all the way home. Over the Jordan, it'll all be different. They speak differently there, and they do things differently. The way they talk, the way they do things, it'll all be a shock to you. It'll be like entering another world. I'll cope, because it's where I grew up. You? You'll be foreigners. Little children will call you names in the street. Older men will call out rude things to you as you go by. You'll be . . . you'll be like fish out of water. You won't be treated the way you deserve, and you both ought to be treated like princesses, the way you've stuck by me through everything.'

She smiles, and then her face grows hard again.

'We've hardly any money, and no one will want to marry you. You'll be poor, and you'll stay poor for the rest of your lives.'

Naomi has tears in her eyes but she keeps talking, willing the words out, knowing that if she stops, she won't be able to say any more.

'And I don't want that for you. I don't want you to be poor. You don't deserve it; no one deserves it. You're lovely girls, and you don't need an old woman to spoil your lives for you . . . so I want to say goodbye here, by the sea.'

She is sobbing, but she's in control.

'I want you to go back to your mothers' homes. Go back to what you used to be before you knew my family. Leave me here. You owe it to yourselves.'

Ruth and Orpah are crying too. They lean forward to hug their mother-in-law, three women in tears on a beach, alone by the sea where nothing can ever live.

'We can't leave you now!' declares Orpah.

'What will you do?' asks Ruth.

'I'll do what I've always done. I'll get by, I always have. I'll have a few family connections left. I'm a survivor.' The older woman has strength and she knows it.

'You shouldn't have to get by!' says Ruth, crossly.

'Young lady, I will and you know it. I'm thinking about your lives now. I'm not going to have any more sons for you to marry. I'm too old to find another husband.' She holds up her worn, lined hands and smiles, sadly. 'Who'd have me?'

She frowns again. 'Life's gone bad for me. They always said my people shouldn't marry outside their own kind. They said our God wouldn't like it. Perhaps he's jealous. I don't know. Your families had their own gods, who you left when you married into mine. You go back to them. Maybe they'll look after you better than my God has.'

Orpah's crying again, but Ruth is angry. You can see it in the way she clenches her fists. Naomi looks up. Coming along the road, in the distance, is a long caravan of traders, good people to tag along with. They are heading back to Moab, probably laden down with foodstuffs to sell at a fat profit. There's a famine in Moab, but as they still say, it's an ill wind that doesn't do anybody any good.*

Naomi leans forward, places a firm but gentle hand on each of the girls' shoulders.

'Now's the time! I love you both, but it's time for you to go! Listen to an old woman who knows! Please . . . please do as I say. It's the right thing to do.'

All three stand. The two girls nod. They hug and kiss their mother-in-law, then start making their way towards the caravan going past. Naomi watches them, then turns away to stare out across the Dead Sea again, her face wet with tears. She can't bear to watch, but knows it's the right thing to do. It's the sensible thing.

She hears footsteps and turns, startled. Who?

It's Ruth, defiantly standing there, almost glaring at her. She speaks. 'I'm not going!' There's a long silence.

'Why?'

'Don't argue. Please! Don't argue! Don't tell me to go away any more, I can't bear it – no, you listen now! It's my turn! Where you go, I'm going to go.

Wherever you stay tonight, I'm staying there too! Your people are going to be my people. Your God is going to be my God now. Where you die, I'll die. Where you're buried, I'm going to be buried, too. And Naomi, I'll say this. I've decided. Only death is going to keep us apart, do you hear me?' More silence, just the gentle evening wind stroking the waves.

She says it again, more softly. 'Naomi? Do you hear me?'

Naomi nods. She holds out a hand and Ruth takes it. They are mother and daughter now. Then, although it's starting to get dark, they hitch up their baggage and step out onto the road again. They want to be filling their water bottles at the River Jordan tomorrow. It's a long way ahead, but it somehow doesn't feel so far now.

UNIT 9

Teacher's notes

Aim To consider the strength that commitment can give to a family.

This episode is taken from the first chapter of the book of Ruth – a short story that initially provides an insight into how a family survives hardship and bereavement, and then develops into a touching tale of human love.

The final words of the book provide a fascinating reason for its inclusion in the Bible: Ruth became the great-grandmother of King David, and if you continue the chronology in Matthew 1.5, a distant ancestor of Jesus of Nazareth.

Prompts A salt shaker. A picture of a deserted beach. A map of Ancient Israel.

Reinforcement of the biblical story

1. Why are each of these three women travelling to Judaea? Imagine you are a reporter who has met them on the beach. (They could be reporting on 'the refugee situation in Moab'.) What would you ask them? Create an interview with them, in which they explain their reasons. In a small group, rehearse and per- form it to the rest of the class, or record it on audiotape.

2. This story hangs around a decision that each of the three women has to make. Naomi, Ruth and Orpah all face a choice, and have to weigh up the consequences before making that choice. In a class or small group discussion, list the 'pros' and 'cons' of the choice for each woman. (Naomi's choice was whether to tell the others to leave her or not.) What would *you* have done in their places?

3. Find out the rest of the story in the book of Ruth in the Bible, and retell it as a photo-story in eight 'frames'.

PSE

1. Ruth showed a great deal of commitment to Naomi. What is commitment? With a partner, try to arrive at a definition. Then think of some situations that call for somebody to be really committed. Write about some examples: 'You know somebody's really committed to _____ when they _____'.

2. Many commitments start with a promise, such as the one Ruth made to Naomi. Can you think of some situations where people make promises before they start something new? With a partner, think of a club that you would like to start. What commitment will you ask for from each of the members? Create a list of club rules that all would have to sign. What do other members of your club think of your rules? Would it be worth being a member?

3. Commitments allow people to trust each other more, if the commitment is shared by all the people involved. What promises would you like parents to make to children? (Remember, what you'd like may not be what you need!) What promises do you think children should make to parents?

4. Find out what people promise each other in a marriage service. Some people like to create their own sets of promises before getting married. What promises would you want someone to make to you if they wanted to be a really close friend with you? What promises do you think you should make?

Literacy work

1. This story is written in the present tense. This means it is all described while it is still happening. Most stories are written in the past tense, describing events as if they happened in the past. How does describing it in the present change the 'feel' of a story? Take a paragraph of description in the story and re-write it in the past tense. Some words will have to change!

2. The setting in this story is particularly bleak. List the ways in which it is described. How do you think the setting of this story affects the way you imagine it in your head? Suppose the main conversation between Naomi and the others took place in a busy market place in the middle of an ancient town, or at a busy harbour, instead of an empty beach. What would be different? Re-write the opening part of the story up to the point where Naomi first speaks, placing it in that setting. How will you convey the sights, sounds and smells of the scene that the three women are walking into?

3. Read the poem 'A family can' (see p. 90). List all the words that are supposed to rhyme together. Can you see any 'false rhymes', which don't actually rhyme? Do you think they work anyway? Why?

Quietly clap the rhythm as you read one verse and the chorus. See if you can detect other rhythms – it's based on an African drumbeat. Some of the beats are quicker than others, which means that some of the words are meant to be said faster than others. Can you see where? Can you play the rhythm of the poem on percussion instruments? Plan a performance of the poem with percussion, allowing space between each verse to play a repeating pattern of beats.

On the beach

WORKSHEET 1

Name_____ **Date**_____

Read or listen to the story.

Why are Ruth, Naomi and Orpah travelling? Write your answers underneath their faces.

What decisions do they make on the beach? Write your answers in the boxes on the right.

Naomi

_____

_____

Orpah

_____

_____

Ruth

_____

_____

On the beach

WORKSHEET 2

Name_____ **Date**_____

Study this version of Ruth's words to Naomi, from Ruth 1.16-17.

Don't ask me to leave you
Or turn back from you
Wherever you go
I will go
Wherever you stay
I will stay
Your people will be my people
And your God will be my God
Wherever you die I will die
And there will I be buried
May God punish me
If anything but Death comes between us.

Read and learn the speech, sharing out parts of it among a small group, preparing for a group performance.

Annotate (mark on this sheet) the places where you will have to:

● show a particular expression on your face;

● use particular gestures;

● speak more quietly or loudly.

Remember that you are trying to convey a sense of *commitment* of one person for another.

UNIT 10

Poet's corner

Poetry resources for use with the other nine units

Joseph
When Joseph in his shiny clothes
Spoke far too much, his brothers rose
And sold him into slavery –
He dropped out of their family.

Instead, he rose to heights unknown,
The power behind the Pharaoh's throne
Was his, he thought that he was free –
He didn't need his family.

Or so he thought, until the day
Some foreign merchants came to pay
For grain. In shock, he turned to see,
The brothers of his family.

The years flashed back – at first, in rage,
He locked his brothers in a cage –
But hatched a plan that probably
Would help and heal his family.

For what they'd cursed had turned to good.
He'd now grown wise and understood
That when you can forgive, you're free –
To live in peace as family.

Ice

I heard her say she hates me.
I hate her through and through.
We both were friends at half past one
But now it's half past two.

She's cruel and mean and nasty,
A creature born of hell.
She has a whinging whining voice
And spots to match as well.

It happened after playtime.
I soon was seeing red,
But now I wish I hadn't used
The nasty words I said.

I hope that she'll forgive me,
And I'll forgive her too.
But how can we start talking?
I don't know what to do!

Eric the wolf cub

The rain fell as soft as the kiss of a mother
The trees dripped with tears of love from a father
The wind whipped the branches like waves typhoon-tossed
And poor little Eric the wolf cub was lost.
It had started so easy that warm summer night
With the stars winking 'Do it!' he'd tiptoed outside
Full of anger at brothers who'd laughed at his size
He'd show them! He'd sort it! They'd all realize!
He'd run in the forest as head of the pack
With the wind in his fur and the sun on his back
Hunting caribou, buffalo, bison and bear!
He'd bring them all down, drag them back to his lair!
He'd tear them apart with his shining white teeth!
But his anger had hidden the fear underneath.
The forest was wetter and darker than hell since
He'd left the old haunts that his pack knew so well
His nerves were in tatters, he'd started to find
That each rustle of branches, each movement behind
Was a portent of danger – his nostrils now flared

The bears would be hunting – and Eric was scared.
It's one thing to dream of amazing adventure
In shelter and warmth that your parents have lent you
It's easy imagining life's a big lark
It's not when you take your first steps in the dark
Into strangeness and terror and mind-numbing fear
To make your own way when the path's so unclear
What was normal grows strange at the first hint of pain
And Eric's young courage dissolved in the rain.
He climbed up a valley, deep shadowed in death
Eyes widened in terror and struggling for breath
So sure he was hunted by something that in a
Short while would be having this wolf cub for dinner.
At last, as the storm was abating he spied
A small cave in the distance and scrambled inside
It seemed to be empty, so lonely and wet
He lay down, quite grateful for all he could get.
Bedraggled, and soaking, he sank to the floor
He dozed for a time, woke, then slept a bit more
As the sky cracked with lightning, he longed to go back
To the smell of his parents, his brothers, his pack.
Sometime later, he woke, and was frozen in fright, for
Something had entered his cave in the night
His eyes wide in panic, his mind quickly spun
To fight or to fly? There was nowhere to run.
The shadow moved closer – he tightened his breath
Eric the wolf cub prepared for his death
The creature leaned forward, it sniffed him, then halted
'Don't hurt me!' whined Eric. His father just snorted
'Hurt you? I ought to, you silly young whelp
We've all been out searching, with everyone's help
I'm glad that we've found you, but don't start to shout
We'd better get home as the bears are about!'
He led the way back with his son close behind
Feeling stupid and selfish and thoughtless and blind
To the love that his family had in its heart
Perhaps it was better to make a new start.
The moral is simple to any young dope:
Don't try to leave home 'till you're certain to cope.

(The letters on the right signify the rhyming scheme for this kind of sonnet. The metre has five beats on each line. These enable emphasis of certain words.)

A sonnet for a rabbit

I was with him when his small life ended	a
One moment he was breathing, and then was still	b
Nothing about him could now be mended	a
No strong medicine, no magic pill	b
Would mend the sickness, for his large dark eyes	c
Had lost their light, the life that made him glorious	d
In my sight, and then to my surprise	c
His limbs, whose speed had once been notorious	d
Grew stiff. I stroked the long hair, so dark, so smooth,	e
And held him as once I used to do	f
Not for my comfort, not my grief to soothe	e
But to say goodbye to someone whose life I knew	f
To you, he was just a rabbit, whose life was at an end	g
But he was my companion, and my best friend.	g

The monster

I want to smash, I want to roar
And kick my way out through the door
And tower above the neighbourhood
(I'm sick to death of being good!)
I'll put my fists through roofs and walls
And screw up cars in metal balls
And kick my feet through steel and granite
And stamp my feet to shake the planet
With earthquake, storm and tidal wave
(I'll show them how to misbehave!)
For everyone will come to see
My anger, in this world, set free.
They'll call the Army, ring the Police
And pray my anger won't increase
To blow this world to kingdom come –
So make my bedtime *later*, Mum!

The joy of mealtimes together

The answer's no.
If I've told you once, I've told you a thousand times.
No you can't.
Because I've said so. You should have gone when I told you to go.
Can't you wait?
I've told you to wait.
Oh all right then, but you'd better hurry.
Come on!
Where've you been?
Did you remember to wash your hands?
Good, now hurry up and eat your meal!
And sit up in that chair!
Of course it's cold, you've been taking ages to eat it!
And if you don't finish it, there'll be no pudding.
Yes, I do mean it.
Don't glare at me like that.
Now get on.
Don't make faces at your sister either.
And don't you join in. Sit still!
Pardon? Oh.
On the floor? Where?
I think I'm getting one of my headaches.

The kiss

When you are small you often miss
The things that go to make a kiss
For when I fell and cut my knee
Mum kissed the pain away from me.
My nightmare dreams of eyes and teeth
She kissed and stroked to gentle sleep.
The day that bullies taught me fear
She kissed away the angry tears.
I never knew the love that's spent
On parenthood until I went
And had some children of my own –
A kiss still says you're not alone
A kiss can heal the hurt that all
This world can give an infant small.
It says 'I care.' It says 'Be strong.'
A kiss can say we all belong
Together, for the truth is this –
We're all connected when we kiss.

Heredity

My grandfather gave me his eyebrows,
My earlobes descend from my mum,
My squint is the same as my granny's,
My father donated his tum.
My cleverness comes from my teacher,
So somebody answer my plea –
If most of this came from the others,
Then which is the bit that is me?

(*The poem below is intended to work as a performance piece, with different groups taking on different parts. The refrain 'Discontented murmurs, murmurs of discontent' could serve as an introduction that starts as a whisper, then builds to a crescendo.*)

Discontented murmurs

(*Children*)
We're tired of all your stupid rules,
And things you say we ought to wear,
The films we're not allowed to watch,
The way you want to style our hair!
Our music makes you sulk and frown?
You always shout to *turn it down*!
We're tired of you, we're tired of life,
So listen to our lament!
Discontented murmurs, murmurs of discontent!

(*Parents*)
You say we moan, but don't you care?
We have to wash your underwear!
We brought you up, we helped you grow,
Although it's hard you ought to know
One day you'll wish you'd listened!
One morning you'll repent!
Your discontented murmurs, murmurs of discontent!

(*Narrator*)
This battle's been running for ages,
It can't be a game that they choose,
'Cause nobody wants to surrender,
And everyone's frightened to lose.
If parents try not to frustrate their kids,
And children just try to obey,

Then something more healthy can happen,
And nobody's needing to say,
They're tired of this, they're tired of that,
One hundred and one per cent,
Their discontented murmurs, murmurs of discontent.

Albert and the roller coaster

One summer, when trade had gone quiet,
It happened, as happens to most,
That Mr and Mrs Ramsbottom
Took another day out at the coast.
Young Albert could come, they decided,
As he had nothing better to do,
But this time he'd have to stay with them,
And best keep away from the zoo.
He remembered to bring his stick with him,
For pointing and poking between.
It still had its horse's-head handle,
With some bite marks to show where it'd been.
At the beach they all had a quick paddle,
While the sea was a shimmering haze.
Then Father got stung by a jellyfish,
And said words it ain't proper to say.
So they all took a break at the funfair,
Where Albert's young eyes opened wide,
At the height of the new roller coaster,
And he knew that he wanted a ride.
But his parents said they would have none of it,
For their son was too easily led.
So they all went instead on the roundabout,
'Till his mother's face flushed a deep red.
Perhaps it was turning that did it.
She had to dismount and sit down.
But when Father returned with a strong cup of tea,
Their son was nowhere to be found.
He'd made straightaway for the coaster,
And queued up to take a quick ride.
Having done that, he felt disappointed,
That no one had dropped out, or cried.
But during a go on the coconuts,
He noticed, in middle of game,
His stick with its horse's-head handle

Had gone, to the little lad's shame.
His search took him back to the coaster,
Where he watched it climb up to the stars.
As it fell, he remembered, his stick had been placed,
On the floor of the very first car.
But the attendant in charge would have none of it.
Albert left with a flea in his ear.
But he wanted his stick, and would have it.
His rage cost the little lad dear.
He sneaked in behind the control room.
Climbing over a fence with great care,
But his collar got snagged as the coaster swung round,
And Albert swung up through the air.
He started to yell rather loudly,
In the hope they would hear him below.
'Have you paid for that ride?' a man shouted,
'Or is it the acrobat show?'
The little lad's plight was soon noticed,
By a policeman who pointed it out.
He was just extricating his notebook,
When Albert, he fell with a shout.
The engines that drive roller coasters,
Have sprockets, and cables, and teeth.
Young Albert fell right in the motor,
That was turning and winding beneath.

The hospital made a great effort,
With sewing, and tying, and stuff.
They transplanted bits on to pieces,
But they still couldn't do well enough.
So young Albert they placed in a jam jar,
And returned him, with stick, to his mum,
Who placed them on dining-room mantelpiece,
As a warning to all who would come.
'Our Albert, he never would listen!
His absences left us so vexed!
At least where he is, he's no trouble,
As he was from one day to the next!'
The lesson, dear children, is simple.
For a long life that's brimming with health,
Your parents know best, so obey them,
If you don't want to end on the shelf.

I want

'I want to go on the beach today!'
'And I want to go to the fair!'
'I want to climb a big mountain!'
'And I want to sit in my chair!'
'I want to play in amusement arcades!'
'And I want to sail in the breeze!
But if somebody here doesn't compromise,
Then NOBODY's going to be pleased!'

(This is intended to work as a performance piece for a number of voices with percussion.)

A family can

A family can, a family will,
A family does what it has to,
Respecting the old, and raising the young,
And bringing them up to be close to,
[Each other, your brother,
Your sister or father or mother]   *(repeat once)*

Whether you're old, or whether you're young,
Top of the ladder or bottom,
Still got a face, still got a place,
Even if you have forgotten,
Each other . . .

Family loves, and family hurts,
Family life can be murder,
Have to be hard, have to be strong,
Stretching your love even further,
Each other . . .

Family works, as family can,
When everyone learns to remember,
Keep on forgiving as long as you're living
From January through to December,
Each other . . .

APPENDIX 1
Strong feelings

A teacher sometimes has to take on the role of a counsellor. Children can become extremely distressed in class, sometimes because of a trauma being experienced at home, and sometimes because of unresolved fears or hurts that have been simmering quietly for months. The classroom isn't the best place for sorting out these things, and very few teachers have the time, experience or training to offer more than gentle encouragement to a child facing a difficult situation. It is very easy to say the wrong thing, and then place yourself or the child in further dilemmas involving trust and inappropriateness of the relationship.

However, school is a more neutral environment than many, and that gentle word of encouragement from someone outside the family situation can make a lot of difference to a child who thinks that nobody understands and that no one cares. The curriculum also allows for a healthy exploration of personal, social and moral issues, which can aid the child by increasing their understanding, and certain lessons can provide a place where strong feelings can be expressed in a positive, sensitively controlled environment.

What follows is designed to be of use to the teacher facing this kind of situation. Perhaps a child has walked in with a problem. Perhaps the lesson material sparked off something. You may want to be of some help, but you *must* be aware that:

- your school will have policies dealing with pastoral issues and Child Protection. Whatever support you lend a child (including confidentiality) has to be in line with them;

- for your own protection, do not allow the situation to arise, where you are alone in a room with a distressed child, allowing the possibility at some future date of your being made the subject of an allegation.

Bereavement and loss

If a child seeks you out to talk, be supportive, be available, and really listen.

Be prepared to face and possibly share your own feelings about loss and bereavement.

Say that it is all right to cry, to be sad, to be angry, and that it is even all right to smile in these situations. Explain that it sometimes takes a long time to get over sadness, but gradually everyone begins to feel better.

Explain that talking about your feelings with someone you trust can sometimes help.

Ensure that your colleagues (including the Head) are all aware, so that no one distresses the child with an unintended inappropriate remark. It may be that there is someone with more experience of the child or of the problem, who can offer support to you or to the child.

Encourage a small circle of close friends to support the child.

Be prepared for the expression of grief. It may take the form of withdrawal, aggressiveness, panic, anxiety, anger, guilt, fear, regression and symptoms of bodily distress. Be understanding, but try not to single out the grieving child for special privileges or compensations – be kind and understanding, but encourage them to function as a member of class. They may have shortened attention spans and have trouble concentrating, but the work may be a relief to them.

Suggest ways of positively celebrating the life of the person who has died. A scrapbook is one way – you may think of others appropriate to the child.

Communicate with the parents. Keep them informed of the child's progress.

Your school may have useful information, some of it child-centred, on how grief and loss can be faced. If not, or if you think your school needs more input, contact:

Cruse – Bereavement Care

126 Sheen Road, Richmond, Surrey TW9 1UR   Tel: 0181 940 4818

The Compassionate Friends

53 North Street, Bristol BS3 1EN   Tel: 0117 9539 639

Do not isolate or insulate children from death in your normal curriculum. It is part of the natural life cycle, and should be discussed, not covered up.

Dealing with anger

Anger is a vital passion. It can be a valuable personal asset. There are times when anger can be an entirely right and proper response to a situation. It can also, wrongly handled, be the factor that makes a situation worse. Correctly handled, it may be the factor that eventually leads to the situation being made better.

If a child is angry, encourage them first of all to face it, and not just blame it on someone or something else. A child may be extremely angry while remaining unaware of it, expressing the feelings in another, apparently unrelated way.

Healthy anger is a response to injustice – unhealthy anger is a lashing out when feeling personally threatened. Distinguishing between the two is often difficult, which is why 'controlling' measures can help – they make space for considering what is actually going on. Helpful advice to a child about controlling anger may include:

- removing yourself physically from the person or situation that is making you angry;

- expressing the anger by talking about it to someone you trust, untangling actual threats from imagined ones;

- writing it down. Use this to ask yourself whether it was actually worth getting that angry in the first place. If the anger keeps recurring, then keep an anger diary, noting down the times and places where it happens, and the way you reacted;

- channel the energy into another strenuous activity (running, swimming, punching a pillow . . .);

- consciously relaxing (take a long hot bath, stroke your pet rabbit, watch some TV, listen to music . . .);

- laughing about it – or crying!

Children need to be told that it is important *not* to make major decisions or judgements about people when you are angry. We have to be careful what we say, as the words can't be called back, shouting doesn't solve things, and it may even become a bad habit. Poorly expressed anger can lose us a friend, and it can make us feel so stupid afterwards that we are left nursing even more regrets.

When a child has calmed down, encourage them to consider the positive steps they can take to make the situation better:

- the child's anger may be rooted in something deeper. The causes of their initial 'flare-ups' may need examining, so that with a little self-knowledge they can anticipate and handle difficult situations more successfully. Some schools operate successful behaviour modification programmes that help children gain a measure of self-control (see *Oh No! Not You Again!*, details below), and your school may have a behaviour policy that can be used to support this. Your Special Needs Co-ordinator may also be of help here;

- if something is wrong, we can do our best to positively resolve the situation without becoming aggressive (i.e. by complaining openly to the person who has offended us, or the people in charge). If the situation cannot be changed, we may have to consider either changing our response to it so we cannot be hurt by it, or removing ourselves from it;

- if a friendship has broken down, then we can decide whether we want to make friends again. This will involve expressing the reason for the anger to that person, and creating a sense of forgiveness (sometimes on all sides) for hurt caused. At some point beyond the injustice or unfairness of a situation, there will be an element of personal hurt to be dealt with. That's where the powerful act of continuing forgiveness can come in, not as a 'forgive and forget', but where somebody can declare that they don't want to hold on to that anger any more – instead, they want and seek a renewal of the broken friendship.

For further reading

Myra Chave-Jones, *Living with Anger*, Triangle Books, 1992 (ISBN 0 281 04571 2). A philosophical and theological exploration of the roots of anger, with practical suggestions for self-help.

Fiona Wallace and Diane Caesar, *Oh No! Not You Again!*, Lucky Duck Publishing, 1998 (ISBN I 873942 95 8). A practical series of strategies and worksheets for enabling children to assess and modify their own playtime behaviour.

Physical neglect or sexual abuse

It may happen that at some point in your career, you will have suspicions that a child in your care is suffering from physical neglect or sexual abuse. Your school will have a Child Protection policy for dealing with this kind of eventuality. Follow it to the letter. Such policies are placed there for the protection of children and staff.

APPENDIX 2

Assessment

While there is no statutory requirement to keep detailed records or evidence of a child's level of attainment in Religious Education, it remains good practice to make some assessment based on learning objectives. This can be formative (a week to week monitoring, providing a useful source of feedback to help with planning future material) and summative (an end of year summary of a child's achievements made on the annual report to parents).

This book has been designed to give children the opportunity to explore issues that are central to the understanding and experience of religion, and their achievements in this field will need to be monitored in line with your locally determined Religious Education syllabus.

Each unit in this book will enable the following areas to be taught and assessed:

Unit 1   A family at war

Aim: to consider anger and envy as strong feelings, and the issues that can cause them, such as insensitivity and lack of 'fairness'. Based on the early life of Joseph, as detailed in Genesis 37.

Unit 2   Payback time

Aim: to study the processes of reconciliation and coping with anger, using events from the later life of Joseph as detailed in Genesis 42.1-24. Best used as a sequel to Unit 1.

Unit 3   Going back

Aim: to consider the importance of celebrating 'coming of age', and of the need for parents to 'let go'. Based on the incident recorded in Luke 2.41-51, when the boy Jesus went missing for three days.

Unit 4   The healer

Aim: to consider the process of grieving, and the support that family members can give each other at times of crisis. Based on the first part of the 'Raising of Lazarus' in John 11.1-43.

Unit 5   The battle

Aim: to consider what it means to 'leave home'. Based on the first part of the parable of the Prodigal Son, as found in Luke 15.11-31.

Unit 6   The ration book

Aim: to look at the parent/child relationship in terms of authority and obedience, and love and understanding, using ideas contained in Paul's letter to the Ephesians 6.1-4.

Unit 7   The quiver of arrows

Aim: to consider the different roles in society and the home assigned to boys and girls. Based on Romans 12.2, Psalm 127 and Proverbs 31.10-31.

Unit 8   Homework

Aim: to consider practical ways of showing love, in the light of 1 Corinthians 13.

Unit 9   On the beach

Aim: to consider the strength that commitment can give to a family, based on the first chapter of the book of Ruth.

The following self-assessment sheets are designed to help the teacher with measuring a child's attainment in any of the units. Many teachers find that self-assessment encourages children to take more interest in their own learning. At the beginning of (or during) the teaching of a topic, it awakens the child to the issues being studied, and at the end of a topic, it enables the child to show what has been learned.

The first worksheet is designed for formative assessment (to use at the beginning, or as part of a topic) and is of a fairly general nature, intended to give you a picture of a child's understanding of 'family'.

The second worksheet is summative – designed to provide you with a child's perception of how that topic (and their understanding) has progressed.

Families

1. What is a family?

2. Why do you think people live in families?

3. What are the good things about your family?

4. What do you think are the most important rules for living in a happy family?

5. Either:
   - draw your family here, with some objects that each person uses; or
   - design a coat of arms for your family, with symbols for each member of your family.

Name_____ **(2)**

Families

1. Name the story (or stories) that you have studied as part of this topic.

2. Which story did you enjoy best? Why? What was the most important thing that you learned from this story? (What did it have to say about living in a family?)

3. Think about all the pieces of work that you did in this topic:
    ● Which piece of work are you most pleased with? Why?
    ● Was there anything that you found difficult?
    ● Is there one piece of work that you could do again better? How would you improve it?
    ● Is there something you would like to find out more about?

4. During this topic, did you:
    ● Work by yourself all the time?
    ● Share ideas with others?
    ● Ask for help from others?

5. Draw a picture to show something you will always remember from this topic.

APPENDIX 3

Literacy links and the writing of poetry

The following is not an exhaustive list of all the possibilities for promoting development of literacy using this book, but rather a summary of the specific activities suggested in each literacy section. The RE and PSE sections with each unit also contain opportunities for development of reading comprehension if used with photocopied sections of the story, and also provide opportunities for speaking and listening work and drama.

Unit 1   A family at war

Dialogue and monologue as a clue to motivation and character/ using symbolism in poetry.

Unit 2   Payback time

Writing of letters and diaries/ summarizing a passage/ rhyme schemes.

Unit 3   Going back

Reading comprehension/ character study/ re-writing a passage in own words.

Unit 4   The healer

Story structure/ titles/ imaginary interviews/ sonnets/ analysing a poem for meaning.

Unit 5   The battle

Settings for stories/ narrative poetry.

Unit 6 The ration book

Style and viewpoint/ stories with a message/ dramatized reading of poetry/ comparing similar types of poem.

Unit 7 *The quiver of arrows*

Reading comprehension/ thinking about how we learn to read and write/ researching a topic.

Unit 8 *Homework*

Writing free verse using dialogue/ studying points of view in a story/ analysing beat and metre in poetry.

Unit 9 *On the beach*

Writing in different tenses/ use of different settings/ false rhymes and use of rhythm in poetry.

A few thoughts on writing poetry

The best books I've ever encountered on the subject of teaching children how to write poetry are by Sandy Brownjohn (see below), who suggests that children be steered away from the assumption that poems have to rhyme. Many children love rhyme, but lack the skills to handle it well, and their efforts sometimes end up sounding like something that would gladden the heart of the world's worst rhymester, William McGonagle.

However, I do think that rhyme is still worth teaching, and would suggest the following if you want to take it further with children.

First give them practice at handling metre (or beat), by studying the number of 'feet' (or beats) in a line. Wordsworth (the boat scene from *The Prelude* Book 1, from line 357) and Shakespeare (St Crispian's Day speech from *Henry V)* are good for examples that don't rhyme. Read out examples, and discuss which words are the ones that carry the beat in a line. Children can also develop a sense of beat by comparing different poetic forms in a non-sense language to see how the beats work. A limerick would start, 'Da dadda da dadda da dadda . . .' and so on. Underline examples for display. ('Can *you* spot the words that carry the beat?') Limit the selection of forms, and then move on to 'rhyme'.

Brainstorm and provide lists of words that rhyme, and have children working in twos with a set of provided rhyming words and a set poetic format (such as a limerick) to see which 'team' can produce the best poem. Highlight successful examples when 'feeding back' afterwards. Keep emphasizing the importance of metre, and positively discuss the way that some constructions just don't work, mentioning that even the best poets have 'off days'! Then move the more successful on to something a little more complex, such as a sonnet. Those who struggle with writing poetry may be helped if you can provide a suitable 'last line', which will give them something to 'work towards'

– steal some from published poems, and afterwards, see how your class efforts match up to the original. Try this with famous first lines as well (Blake's *The Tiger*) and prepare for hilarity. Place unfinished poems on a noticeboard in class, and invite other children to try and finish them.

Useful reading

Sandy Brownjohn, *Does It Have to Rhyme?* Hodder and Stoughton, 1980, ISBN 0 340 25514 5

What Rhymes With Secret? Hodder and Stoughton, 1982, ISBN 0 340 2827 1

Rosalind Fergusson, *The Penguin Rhyming Dictionary*, Penguin, 1984. Indispensable for giving you word lists, but not to be actually handled by children because of some of the 'adult' content. ISBN 014 051 136 9

E.O. Parrott (ed.), *How to Be Well-Versed in Poetry*, Penguin, 1990. A useful (if vulgar) guide to a wide range of poetic forms, told with memorable humour. ISBN 0 14 01 1275 8

APPENDIX 4

Fitting the units into your RE syllabus

How will the units from this book fit into your local or regional syllabus for Religious Education, of which there is such a variety? Listed below are 'trigger words' relating to each unit, which you may find helpful when looking for links with your own syllabus.

As you might expect, *all* of these units are intended to cover work relating to:

> Family/Relationships and Moral Values/Moral Values and Attitudes/Sacred Writings

What follows is in addition to the above.

Unit 1   A family at war

Old Testament/Bible stories/key figures/reconciliation/forgiveness

Unit 2   Payback time

Old Testament/Bible stories/key figures/reconciliation/forgiveness

Unit 3   Going back

Jesus/Son of God/childhood of Jesus/New Testament stories/celebrations/initiation ceremonies/significant moments

Unit 4   The healer

Miracles of Jesus/New Testament stories/death and bereavement/ultimate questions

Unit 5   The battle

Parables of Jesus/New Testament stories/Fatherhood of God/forgiveness/repentance

Unit 6   The ration book

Authority/obedience/responsibility

Unit 7   The quiver of arrows

Old Testament texts/gender

Unit 8   Homework

New Testament stories/anger

Unit 9   On the beach

Key figures/Old Testament stories/commitment

APPENDIX 5

Bible passages

Photocopiable for use with the units

Joseph and his brothers (Genesis 37.1-35)

Jacob continued to live in the land of Canaan, where his father had lived, and this is the story of Jacob's family.

Joseph, a young man of seventeen, took care of the sheep and goats with his brothers, the sons of Bilhah and Zilpah, his father's concubines. He brought bad reports to his father about what his brothers were doing.

Jacob loved Joseph more than all his other sons, because he had been born to him when he was old. He made a long robe with full sleeves for him. When his brothers saw that their father loved Joseph more than he loved them, they hated their brother so much that they would not speak to him in a friendly manner.

One night Joseph had a dream, and when he told his brothers about it, they hated him even more. He said, 'Listen to the dream I had. We were all in the fields tying up sheaves of wheat, when my sheaf got up and stood up straight. Yours formed a circle round mine and bowed down to it.'

'Do you think you are going to be a king and rule over us?' his brothers asked. So they hated him even more because of his dreams and because of what he said about them.

Then Joseph had another dream and said to his brothers, 'I had another dream, in which I saw the sun, the moon, and eleven stars bowing down to me.'

He also told the dream to his father, and his father scolded him: 'What kind of a dream is that? Do you think that your mother, your brothers, and I are going to come and bow down to you?' Joseph's brothers were jealous of him, but his father kept thinking about the whole matter.

One day when Joseph's brothers had gone to Shechem to take care of their father's flock, Jacob said to Joseph, 'I want you to go to Shechem, where your brothers are taking care of the flock.'

Joseph answered, 'I am ready.'

His father said, 'Go and see if your brothers are safe and if the flock is all right; then come back and tell me.' So his father sent him on his way from the Valley of Hebron.

Joseph arrived at Shechem and was wandering about in the country when a man saw him and asked him, 'What are you looking for?'

'I am looking for my brothers, who are taking care of their flock,' he answered. 'Can you tell me where they are?'

The man said, 'They have already left. I heard them say that they were going to Dothan.' So Joseph went after his brothers and found them at Dothan.

They saw him in the distance, and before he reached them, they plotted against him and decided to kill him. They said to one another, 'Here comes that dreamer. Come on now, let's kill him and throw his body into one of the dry wells. We can say that a wild animal killed him. Then we will see what becomes of his dreams.'

Reuben heard this and tried to save Joseph. 'Let's not kill him,' he said. 'Just throw him into this well in the wilderness, but don't hurt him.' He said this, planning to save him from them and send him back to his father. When Joseph came up to his brothers, they ripped off his long robe with full sleeves. Then they took him and threw him into the well, which was dry.

While they were eating, they suddenly saw a group of Ishmaelites travelling from Gilead to Egypt. Their camels were loaded with spices and resins. Judah said to his brothers, 'What will we gain by killing our brother and covering up the murder? Let's sell him to these Ishmaelites. Then we won't have to hurt him; after all, he is our brother, our own flesh and blood.' His brothers agreed, and when some Midianite traders came by, the brothers pulled Joseph out of the well and sold him for twenty pieces of silver to the Ishmaelites, who took him to Egypt.

When Reuben came back to the well and found that Joseph was not there, he tore his clothes in sorrow. He returned to his brothers and said, 'The boy is not there! What am I going to do?'

Then they killed a goat and dipped Joseph's robe in its blood. They took the robe to their father and said, 'We found this. Does it belong to your son?'

He recognized it and said, 'Yes, it is his! Some wild animal has killed him. My son Joseph has been torn to pieces!' Jacob tore his clothes in sorrow and put on sackcloth. He mourned for his son a long time. All his sons and daughters came to comfort him, but he refused to be comforted and said, 'I will go down to the world of the dead still mourning for my son.' So he continued to mourn for his son Joseph.

Joseph's brothers go to Egypt to buy corn (Genesis 42.1-24)

When Jacob learnt that there was corn in Egypt, he said to his sons, 'Why don't you do something? I hear that there is corn in Egypt; go there and buy some to keep us from starving to death.' So Joseph's ten half-brothers went to buy corn in Egypt, but Jacob did not send Joseph's full-brother Benjamin with them, because he was afraid that something might happen to him.

The sons of Jacob came with others to buy corn, because there was famine in the land of Canaan. Joseph, as governor to the land of Egypt, was selling corn to people from all over the world. So Joseph's brothers came and bowed down before him with their faces to the ground. When Joseph saw his brothers he recognized them, but he acted as if he did not know them. He asked them harshly, 'Where do you come from?'

'We have come from Canaan to buy food,' they answered.

Although Joseph recognized his brothers, they did not recognize him. He remembered the dreams he had dreamt about them and said, 'You are spies; you have come to find out where our country is weak.'

'No sir,' they answered. 'We have come as your slaves, to buy food. We are all brothers. We are not spies, sir, we are all honest men.'

Joseph said to them, 'No! You have come to find out where our country is weak.'

They said, 'We were twelve brothers in all, sir, sons of the same man in the land of Canaan. One brother is dead, and the youngest is now with our father.'

'It is just as I said,' Joseph answered. 'You are spies. This is how you will be tested: I swear by the name of the king that you will never leave unless your youngest brother comes here. One of you must go and get him. The rest of you will be kept under guard until the truth of what you say can be tested. Otherwise, as sure as the king lives, you are spies.' Then he put them in prison for three days.

On the third day, Joseph said to them, 'I am a God-fearing man, and I will spare your lives on one condition. To prove that you are honest, one of you will stay in the prison where you have been kept; the rest of you may go and take back to your starving families the corn that you have bought. Then you must bring your youngest brother to me. This will prove that you have been telling the truth, and I will not put you to death.'

They agreed to this and said to one another, 'Yes, now we are suffering the consequences of what we did to our brother; we saw the great trouble he was in when he begged for help, but we would not listen. That is why we are in this trouble now.'

Reuben said, 'I told you not to harm the boy, but you wouldn't listen. And now we are being paid back for his death.' Joseph understood what they said, but they did not know it, because they had been speaking to him through an interpreter. Joseph left them and began to cry. When he was able to speak again, he came back, picked out Simeon, and had him bound in front of them.

The boy Jesus in the Temple (Luke 2.41-52)

Every year the parents of Jesus went to Jerusalem for the Passover Festival. When Jesus was twelve years old, they went to the festival as usual. When the festival was over, they started back home, but the boy Jesus stayed in Jerusalem. His parents did not know this; they thought that he was with the group, so they travelled a whole day and then started looking for him among their relatives and friends. They did not find him, so they went back to Jerusalem looking for him. On the third day they found him in the Temple, sitting with the Jewish teachers, listening to them and asking questions. All who heard him were amazed at his intelligent answers. His parents were astonished when they saw him, and his mother said to him, 'My son, why have you done this to us? Your father and I have been terribly worried trying to find you.'

He answered them, 'Why did you have to look for me? Didn't you know that I had to be in my Father's house?' But they did not understand his answer.

So Jesus went back with them to Nazareth, where he was obedient to them. His mother treasured all these things in her heart. Jesus grew both in body and in wisdom, gaining favour with God and men.

The death of Lazarus (John 11.1, 3, 5-7, 17, 20-44)

A man named Lazarus, who lived in Bethany, was ill. Bethany was the town where Mary and her sister lived . . . The sisters sent Jesus a message: 'Lord, your dear friend is ill.'. . . Jesus loved Martha and her sister and Lazarus. Yet when he received the news that Lazarus was ill, he stayed where he was for two more days. Then he said to the disciples, 'Let us go back to Judaea.'. . .

When Jesus arrived, he found that Lazarus had been buried four days before . . . When Martha heard that Jesus was coming, she went out to meet him, but Mary stayed in the house. Martha said to Jesus, 'If you had been here, Lord, my brother would not have died! But I know that even now God will give you whatever you ask him for.'

'Your brother will rise to life,' Jesus told her.

'I know,' she replied, 'that he will rise to life on the last day.'

Jesus said to her, 'I am the resurrection and the life. Whoever believes in me will live, even though he dies; and whoever lives and believes in me will never die. Do you believe this?'

'Yes, Lord!' she answered. 'I do believe that you are the Messiah, the Son of God, who was to come into the world.'

After Martha said this, she went back and called her sister Mary privately. 'The Teacher is here,' she told her, 'and is asking for you.' When Mary heard this, she got up and hurried out to meet him. (Jesus had not yet arrived in the village, but was still in the place where Martha had met him.) The people who were in the house with Mary, comforting her, followed her when they saw her get up and hurry out. They thought that she was going to the grave to weep there.

Mary arrived where Jesus was, and as soon as she saw him, she fell at his feet. 'Lord,' she said, 'if you had been here, my brother would not have died!'

Jesus saw her weeping, and he saw how the people who were with her were weeping also; his heart was touched, and he was deeply moved. 'Where have you buried him?' he asked them.

'Come and see, Lord,' they answered.

Jesus wept. 'See how much he loved him!' the people said.

But some of them said, 'He gave sight to the blind man, didn't he? Could he not have kept Lazarus from dying?'

Deeply moved once more, Jesus went to the tomb, which was a cave with a stone placed at the entrance. 'Take the stone away!' Jesus ordered.

Martha, the dead man's sister, answered, 'There will be a bad smell, Lord. He has been buried four days!'

Jesus said to her, 'Didn't I tell you that you would see God's glory if you believed?' They took the stone away. Jesus looked up and said, 'I thank you, Father, that you listen to me. I know that you always listen to me, but I say this for the sake of the people here, so that they will believe that you sent me.'

After he had said this, he called out in a loud voice, 'Lazarus, come out!'

He came out, his hands and feet wrapped in grave clothes, and with a cloth round his face. 'Untie him,' Jesus told them, 'and let him go.'

The lost son (Luke 15.11-32)

Jesus went on to say, 'There was once a man who had two sons. The younger one said to him, "Father, give me my share of the property now." So the man divided his property between his two sons. After a few days the younger son sold his part of the property and left home with the money. He went to a country far away, where he wasted his money in reckless living. He spent everything he had. Then a severe famine spread over that country, and he was left without a thing. So he went to work for one of the citizens of that country, who sent him out to his farm to take care of the pigs. He wished he could fill himself with the bean pods the pigs ate, but no one gave him anything to eat. At last he came to his senses and said, "All my father's hired workers have more than they can eat, and here I am about to starve! I will get up and go to my father and say, Father, I have sinned against God and against you. I am no longer fit to be called your son; treat me as one of your hired workers." So he got up and started back to his father.

'He was still a long way from home when his father saw him; his heart was filled with pity, and he ran, threw his arms round his son, and kissed him. "Father," the son said, "I have sinned against God and against you. I am no longer fit to be called your son." But the father called his servants. "Hurry!" he said. "Bring the best robe and put it on him. Put a ring on his finger and shoes on his feet. Then go and get the prize calf and kill it, and let us celebrate with a feast! For this son of mine was dead, but now he is alive; he was lost, but now he has been found." And so the feasting began.

'In the meantime the elder son was out in the field. On his way back, when he came close to the house, he heard the music and dancing. So he called one of the servants and asked him, "What's going on?" "Your brother has come back home," the servant answered, "and your father has killed the prize calf, because he got him back safe and sound."

'The elder brother was so angry that he would not go into the house; so his father came out and begged him to come in. But he answered his father, "Look, in all these years I have worked for you like a slave, and I have never disobeyed your orders. What have you given me? Not even a goat for me to have a feast with my friends! But this son of yours wasted all your property on prostitutes, and when he comes back home, you kill the prize calf for him!" "My son," the father answered, "you are always here with me, and everything I have is yours. But we had to celebrate and be happy, because your brother was dead, but now he is alive; he was lost, but now he has been found."'

Children and parents (Ephesians 6.1-4)

Children, it is your Christian duty to obey your parents, for this is the right thing to do. 'Respect your father and your mother' is the first commandment that has a promise added: 'so that all may go well with you, and you may live a long time in the land.'

Parents, do not treat your children in such a way as to make them angry. Instead, bring them up with Christian discipline and instruction.

Children are a gift (Psalm 127.3-5)

Children are a gift from the LORD;
　　they are a real blessing.
The sons a man has when he is young
　　are like arrows in a soldier's hand.
Happy is the man who has many such arrows.
He will never be defeated
　　when he meets his enemies in the place of judgement.

Love (1 Corinthians 13.1-8a)

I may be able to speak the languages of men and even of angels, but if I have no love, my speech is no more than a noisy gong or a clanging bell. I may have the gift of inspired preaching; I may have all knowledge and understand all secrets; I may have all the faith needed to move mountains – but if I have no love, I am nothing. I may give away everything I have, and even give up my body to be burnt – but if I have no love, this does me no good.

Love is patient and kind; it is not jealous or conceited or proud; love is not ill-mannered or selfish or irritable; love does not keep a record of wrongs; love is not happy with evil, but is happy with the truth. Love never gives up; and its faith, hope, and patience never fail.

Love is eternal.

The story of Ruth (Ruth 1.1-18)

Long ago, in the days before Israel had a king, there was a famine in the land. So a man named Elimelech . . . who lived in Bethlehem in Judah, went with his wife Naomi and their two sons Mahlon and Chilion to live for a while in the country of Moab. While they were living there, Elimelech died, and Naomi was left alone with her two sons, who married Moabite girls, Orpah and Ruth. About ten years later Mahlon and Chilion also died, and Naomi was left all alone, without husband or sons.

Some time later Naomi heard that the LORD had blessed his people by giving them a good harvest; so she got ready to leave Moab with her daughters-in-law. They started out together to go back to Judah, but on the way she said to them, 'Go back home and stay with your mothers. May the LORD be as good to you as you have been to me and to those who have died. And may the LORD make it possible for each of you to marry again and have a home.'

So Naomi kissed them good-bye. But they started crying and said to her, 'No! We will go with you to your people.'

'You must go back, my daughters,' Naomi answered. 'Why do you want to come with me? Do you think I could have sons again for you to marry? Go back home, for I am too old to get married again. Even if I thought there was still hope, and so got married tonight and had sons, would you wait until they had grown up? Would this keep you from marrying someone else? No, my daughters, you know that's impossible. The LORD has turned against me, and I feel very sorry for you.'

Again they started crying. Then Orpah kissed her mother-in-law good-bye and went back home, but Ruth held on to her. So Naomi said to her, 'Ruth, your sister-in-law has gone back to her people and to her god. Go back home with her.'

But Ruth answered, 'Don't ask me to leave you! Let me go with you. Wherever you go, I will go; wherever you live, I will live. Your people will be my people, and your God will be my God. Wherever you die, I will die, and that is where I will be buried. May the LORD'S worst punishment come upon me if I let anything but death separate me from you!'

When Naomi saw that Ruth was determined to go with her, she said nothing more.

Together with Children

Together with Children provides practical, topical resource material and information about wider issues in church and school children's work. Its regular features are a real source of inspiration for leaders.

Regular Features:

- a complete all-age service
- stories
- sketches
- activities for special days and festivals
- articles by colleagues in the field of children's work
- reviews of key new resources and books
- a topical feature on a current issue for children's leaders

If you work with the under 12s, we're certain that you'll like it.

Call 0171 898 1499 today to receive your free sample copy.

Together with Children (£1.80 per issue) is published nine times a year and is available from all good Christian bookshops (ISSN 1361-1429), or by subscription. For more details please phone Marie Yateman on 0171 898 1499.

THE NATIONAL SOCIETY
LEADING EDUCATION WITH A CHRISTIAN PURPOSE
REG CHARITY NO. 313070

Few things are more important in the life of any church than the care and nurture of its children. I congratulate those who produce Together with Children *and warmly recommend it as a resource for use by parishes and in children's activities up and down the country.*

ARCHBISHOP OF CANTERBURY

Searching for a sketch for a school assembly or family service?

Look no further than The National Society and Church House Publishing's best-selling drama

Playing Up
Dave Hopwood

Over 30 witty and
thought-provoking sketches
£6.95

0 7151 4895 8

Acting Up
Dave Hopwood

- Raps
- mimes
- monologues
£5.95

0 7151 4866 4

Plays on the Word
Derek Haylock

Nineteen fast-moving,
Bible-based sketches,
including eight for Christmas
£5.95

0 7151 4824 9

Plays for all Seasons
Derek Haylock

A collection of 21 dramas
and plays covering
the whole Christian year
£6.95

0 7151 4884 2

A Fistful of Sketches
Dave Hopwood

Sketches • raps • prayers
• performance poems. Ideal for the
older members of the youth group
£5.95

0 7151 4869 9

All titles above are available from your local Christian bookshop.

The National Society (Church of England) for Promoting Religious Education supports everyone involved in Christian education – teachers, school governors, students, parents, clergy, parish and diocesan education teams – with its legal and professional advice, the resources of its RE centres, courses, conferences and archives.

It is a voluntary Anglican society, also operating ecumenically, and helps to promote inter-faith education and dialogue through its RE centres.

For more details of the Society, or a copy of our current resources catalogue or details on how you can support the continuing work of the Society, please call 0171-898 1499 or email: info@natsoc.c-of-e.org.uk

For more details see our online catalogue: www.chpublishing.co.uk.